THE
NEW YORK
METS
FANS'
BUCKET LIST

MATTHEW CERRONE

TRIUMPH
BOOKS

Library of Congress Cataloging-in-Publication Data

Names: Cerrone, Matthew, author.
Title: The New York Mets Fans' Bucket List / Matthew Cerrone.
Description: Chicago, Illinois : Triumph Books, 2017.
Identifiers: LCCN 2016057523 | ISBN 9781629374093 (paperback)
Subjects: LCSH: New York Mets (Baseball team)—History. | New York Mets
   (Baseball team)—Miscellanea. | BISAC: TRAVEL / United States /
Northeast
   / Middle Atlantic (NJ, NY, PA). | SPORTS & RECREATION /
Baseball / General.
Classification: LCC GV875.N45 C47 2017 | DDC 796.357/64097471—
dc23 LC record available at https://lccn.loc.gov/2016057523

Triumph Books LLC
814 North Franklin Street
Chicago, Illinois 60610
(312) 337-0747
www.triumphbooks.com

Printed in U.S.A.
ISBN: 978-1-62937-409-3
Design by Andy Hansen
Page production by Patricia Frey
Photos courtesy of AP Images unless otherwise noted

To my wife, Dorian, and my daughters, Pria and Tali, I had one thing on my bucket list, and you three filled it. To my mom, Maryjane, who took me to countless Mets games when I was a kid and my dad, Michael, who supported my ideas as an adult. And to Brennan, Stromberg, Verna, and Keenan, it truly does take a village. Thank you all…

Contents

Foreword by David Wright **7**

Chapter 1: Things to Know **11**

#LOLMets **13**

Laugh with the Comedians Who Are Mets Fans **21**

Get Duped by Sidd Finch **26**

Learn About Davey Johnson and the '86 Mets **31**

Understand Why Hodges Belongs in the Hall of Fame **36**

Learn About the Other Mr. Met **41**

Chapter 2: Things to Do **47**

Believe! **49**

Cheer with Cowbell Man **57**

Eat at Citi Field **61**

Attend Mets Fantasy Camp **64**

Fist Bump Mr. Met **68**

Grow a Mustache Like Keith Hernandez **74**

Experience the 7 Line **77**

Learn a Lesson from Bill Buckner **81**

Name Your Kid Shea **86**

Run the Mr. Met Dash **88**

Tour Citi Field **91**

Throw Out the First Pitch **96**

Go to a Playoff Game at Citi Field **99**

Catch a T-Shirt from the Party Patrol **105**

Go to Opening Day **108**

Be Terrific Like Tom Seaver **114**

Enjoy Some New York-Style Piazza **118**

Chapter 3: Places to Go   **125**

Visit Cooperstown   **127**

Go to a Brooklyn Cyclones Game   **130**

Tour the Mets Hall of Fame and Museum   **135**

Meet a Friend at the Apple   **138**

See the Mets on the Road   **141**

Go to Spring Training   **146**

Visit the Bases from Shea   **149**

Chapter 4: Things to Hear   **153**

Get Metsmerized   **155**

Learn Stengelese   **158**

Listen to Bob Murphy   **161**

Meet the Mets   **165**

Chant "Let's Go Mets"   **167**

Chapter 5: Things to Read   **173**

Check Out The Bad Guys Won   **175**

Learn About Alderson in Baseball Maverick   **179**

Click on MetsBlog.com   **183**

Learn the Game from Keith Hernandez's Pure Baseball   **187**

Pick Up a Copy of The Worst Team Money Could Buy   **190**

Relive The Year the Mets Lost Last Place   **192**

Chapter 6: Things to See   **195**

Log On to #MetsTwitter   **197**

Watch Kiner's Korner   **201**

Re-watch 1986 Mets—A Year to Remember *Again and Again*   **205**

Checklist   **211**

Acknowledgments   **215**

Sources   **219**

Foreword

Bobby Valentine yelled into the dugout to me.

I was 18 years old, fresh off being drafted by the Mets, who were kind enough to fly out my family—my three brothers, my mom, and my dad—after I signed. It was my first time in New York, and I had just sat down in the dugout after taking batting practice. "Hey, what are you doing? You think you're going to hit without taking ground balls? Get your glove and get out to third base," Valentine said.

I had never been so nervous to play a game of catch in my life. I had just signed my contract to start my career in the minor leagues and here I am playing catch next to Mike Piazza after my brothers had been pestering him for an autograph. It was my first time at Shea Stadium, and it was just such tremendous motivation for me to get back to play there.

For anybody who doesn't believe that we were a Mets family, I can show them a picture currently framed in my dad's office in Virginia. I couldn't have been more than a couple of years old when it was taken, and the clothes are all outdated—my dad's in stonewash jeans—and he's wearing a Mets hat.

I can't tell you what life would be like without baseball for me. It's given me so much more than I ever could have dreamed, and getting a chance to call Citi Field and Shea Stadium my office is about as great as it gets for a baseball player.

The first time I stepped to the plate at Shea for my first major league at-bat, I did everything I could to breathe deep, remain calm, and soak it all in. However, all I could do was keep sneaking a look at the scoreboard to see myself in a Mets uniform on the Jumbotron.

It's not about just coming to the ballpark and watching a baseball game for Mets fans. Our fans know the game. They know when you do something well—even if it's something that doesn't show up in the box score. They also know when you didn't get the job done because it's about more than just wins and losses to them.

When I'm struggling at the plate, I get thousands of hitting coaches talking to me on the streets of New York. They want to know you as a person, as a player. They want to offer advice, and I do try to listen. There's a visible passion I feel when stopped on the street, and they think they can genuinely help you out by fixing your swing because they've been watching you since you were 18 years old. This speaks to the intensity for baseball in New York.

During the World Series in 2015, I would occasionally glance up for a few seconds to look over the crowd to see the joy on the faces of Mets fans that had our back for so long. To finally get a chance for them to come to Citi Field and see a World Series game, it was one of the most satisfying feelings that I've ever had as a professional baseball player. My teammates and I were finally playing in the World Series. But the reality is we had 50,000 fans at Citi Field—and countless more at home watching on TV—playing in the World Series with us.

As this book shows, there are so many ways to show love for this organization. I've even checked one thing off my own list by naming my daughter Olivia Shea Wright. I had a lot of memories at Shea, but it's more a tip of the cap to the fans for accepting me the way they have. They've seen me make a ton of errors. They've seen me strike out. But that loyalty is still there. New York is a second home to me, and Shea Stadium is where it all began. Thank you for allowing me to live out my dream on one of the biggest stages in the world. And through *The New York Mets Fans' Bucket List*, you'll learn how to further experience all of the things that make being a Mets fan amazin'.

—David Wright

Bucket Ranking

The items throughout the book are accompanied by one to five bucket symbols—relative to where they rank on a bucket list, with five as the highest. Everything included in this book is worthy of a Mets bucket list; some just rank higher than others in the author's opinion.

Chapter 1

Things to Know

#LOLMets

Bucket Rank: 🗑️ 🗑️ 🗑️ 🗑️ 🗑️

In their 55-season history, the Mets have won two world championships, won six division titles, and reached the postseason nine times. There are 10 other baseball teams that have gone longer without a World Series title than the Mets, but the Mets have a way of doing things that frequently get them mocked, ripped, and ridiculed by all of baseball.

Maybe it's the success of the New York Yankees during the late '90s to early 2000s, which has confused local sports fans and validated the idea that the Mets are the city's redheaded little brother or second-class citizen. Or maybe success and arrogance from the Bronx helped enhance a New York bias that ends up influencing opinions outside of Queens. Or maybe it's the tabloid nature of New York City's print media. Or maybe it's the fact that a dozen beat writers—where most teams have two or three reporters on their tail—compete for stories about the Mets on a daily basis, working to dig up and exploit every little thing the team does. Or maybe it's all of the above.

Or maybe it's actually the Mets.

The truth is the Mets sometimes do things that make even the most optimistic, loyal fan scratch his or her head. It happened so often during their 2009–2014 rebuild, the #LOLMets hashtag was created, shared, and frequently trended on Twitter.

The Mets have done some silly things on field, but so do most teams. I'm pretty sure every big league team has dropped a pop-up to lose a game or had a player miss third base when trying to score from second. They've all made costly errors or forgot the number of outs in an inning. However, it's the off-field moments that make the Mets unique. Here are the 10 best (or worst, depending on your point of view) off-the-field moments from the last 20 years that define what it means to be #LOLMets.

1) Citi Field is criticized for being Ebbets Field 2.0

Citi Field opened its doors in 2009, at which point fans and media were put off by how little blue, orange, and Mets history were present in the building. Instead, with its Jackie Robinson Rotunda, critics said it looked and felt more like a new Ebbets Field, which is where the Brooklyn Dodgers played before leaving for Los Angeles in 1958. Of course, it didn't help that Mets principal owner Fred Wilpon grew up a Dodgers fan, attending games and romanticizing his experiences at Ebbets. In subsequent seasons the Mets eventually made structural and design changes to make Citi Field look and feel more like a home for its team, but it didn't erase how people felt when the building debuted.

2) Hey, All-Star catcher Todd Hundley, go play left field

The Mets traded for Los Angeles Dodgers catcher Mike Piazza in May of 1998. He was (and still is) the greatest hitting catcher of all time. It was a great trade, which transformed the franchise and resulted in back-to-back postseason appearances. The only problem was that when they traded for Piazza, the Mets already had Todd Hundley, who was a fan favorite and two-time All-Star who also held the record for most home runs by a catcher in a single season. To make room for Piazza, the Mets put Hundley in the outfield, where he had never played. It was a total disaster. After the season the Mets traded Hundley to Los Angeles, where—in a weird twist of fate—Piazza started his career several years earlier.

3) Go fish, Rickey

In Game 6 of the 1999 National League Championship Series, while their teammates were fighting for their lives against the Atlanta Braves, Mets outfielders Rickey Henderson and Bobby Bonilla were reportedly playing Go Fish in the clubhouse after being switched out of the game earlier in the night. "Obviously, it's not something you want players to do when you're playing any game, let alone a playoff game," Mets general manager Steve Phillips said when asked about the situation after the series.

Bonilla was eventually released, though he is still on their payroll through 2035 (see below). On the other hand, Henderson was voted 1999's National League Comeback Player of the Year and returned to the organization the following season. However, during a game six weeks into the season, Henderson did his notorious, casual, flashy, home-run trot on a ball that hit the outfield wall and resulted in a single. Henderson was put on outright waivers the next day. He was not claimed, became a free agent, and eventually signed a deal to end the season with the Seattle Mariners. "At some point, when you continue to do the wrong thing and say the wrong thing, you continue to wear out your welcome," Phillips said, when asked about Henderson's release. "We were at the point where we were having to compromise our ideals too many times. When taking everything into account, the offense, defense, and the alternatives we had, and what it does to the fabric of the team, we thought it was the right thing to do."

4) Happy Bobby Bonilla Day!

The Mets are mocked every July 1 for having agreed to pay Bobby Bonilla, who has been retired since 2001, $1.19 million every year through 2035. It's an understandable reaction, though very shortsighted. In 1999 after the infamous card game, the Mets owed Bonilla $5.9 million for the following season, after which he would be a free agent. In an effort to avoid paying him the full amount, they negotiated with his agent, Dennis Gilbert, to attach an 8 percent annual interest rate to the money and defer his payments for 35 years.

In the end with interest, the $5.9 million ends up being $29.8 million, which is why the organization is ripped annually on July 1 by nearly every fan and across more or less every sports media outlet. In addition to paying Bonilla through 2035, the Mets are also making

Bobby Bonilla, who drops a fly ball during a 1993 game, will continue collecting $1.19 million a year through 2035. (AP Images)

similar deferred payments to Bret Saberhagen ($250,000 each year through 2029) and Carlos Beltran ($3.1 million each year through 2018).

5) Bret Saberhagen squirts bleach on reporters

In July of 1993, with the Mets 34–65, Brett Saberhagen put bleach into a water gun and fired it into a room full of New York reporters. It took Saberhagen two weeks to confess to being the culprit. "I am sorry for the accident and the failure to come forward, both of which have obviously hurt the club's relations with the media," Saberhagen later said at a press conference addressing the issue.

The bleach incident occurred the same night Saberhagen confessed to *The New York Times* that he set off firecrackers near a group of reporters in the clubhouse the previous month.

"If the reporters can't take it, forget them," Saberhagen said at the time.

Saberhagen underwent arthroscopic knee surgery later that season, after which he returned to go 14–4 with a 2.74 ERA and make the All-Star team. However, the Mets traded him to the Colorado Rockies during the middle of the next season.

6) Scott Kazmir traded for Victor Zambrano

With the Mets four games under .500 but just seven games out of first place the day before the July 31 non-waiver trade deadline in 2004, interim general manager Jim Duquette traded the team's best prospect and 2002 first-round draft pick, Scott Kazmir, to the Tampa Bay Devil Rays for Victor Zambrano.

A top-rated pitching prospect, the left-handed Kazmir was young, able to throw in the mid-90s. Meanwhile, Zambrano had a live fastball but also a history of injuries and led his league in walks, wild pitches, and hit batsmen the year before. The team's pitching coach, Rick Peterson, reportedly told the Mets before the deal that he could get Zambrano straightened out in "10 minutes."

The trade was panned all across baseball—not because the Mets traded Kazmir—but because experts and fans all believed Duquette could have easily received more than just Zambrano. "First of all, you and some of the critics that have criticized the trade are underestimating the ability of Victor Zambrano. We think this guy has the ability to be a tremendous top of the rotation starter," Duquette told WFAN radio on the night of the trade.

Zambrano ended up pitching in just in 39 games for the Mets. He was 10–14 with a 4.42 ERA, which hardly constitutes a "tremendous top of the rotation starter." His last start in Queens was on May 6,

2006, when he ran off the field in the middle of a start for seemingly no reason. It was announced later in the game the he had suffered a torn flexor tendon in his pitching elbow, which eventually led to his second Tommy John elbow surgery. Zambrano was later non-tendered by the Mets and made a free agent in December 2006 because he was expected to miss most of the next season.

On the other hand, Kazmir made his big league debut a few weeks after being traded to the Rays. In his first five seasons with Tampa Bay, he was considered their ace, going 47–37 with a 3.61 ERA while striking out 783 batters in 723 innings spanning 124 starts. He is still pitching in the major leagues while Zambrano has since retired.

7) Willie Randolph fired in the middle of the night

Willie Randolph managed the Mets to a 9–6 win against the Los Angeles Angels on June 16, 2008, during which general manager Omar Minaya waited back at the team's hotel. It had been 16 months since Randolph was hired by the Mets with a multimillion dollar contract. In that time his team had gone from one win away from a World Series appearance to one of the greatest collapses in baseball.

There had been countless rumors in local reports that Randolph might be fired soon. The Sunday before the team made its way west at 33–35, Randolph told reporters that he had packed his suitcase for the trip but was unsure if he would even get on the plane that night. Still unsure of Randolph's status, Minaya had Randolph fly with the team to Anaheim. Two hours after the Mets won to improve to a game below .500, the Mets announced Randolph's firing, while his family waited for him to come home back in New York.

The press release announcing the move was issued by the team at 3:12 AM—a time when every newspaper was already written and being shipped and nearly all of the team's beat reporters and media were fast asleep. The timing of the decision clearly angered New York's media because they repeatedly made a point in their stories that Randolph had been fired at 3:12 AM, the time they received notification. Naturally, fans picked up on this notion and continued the criticism, seeing it as yet another example of the team's perceived poor judgement.

Of course, Randolph wasn't fired at 3:12 AM Eastern time. He was fired at 12:12 AM Pacific time, which is the time it was in California after the conclusion of the game when managers are typically given bad news. In addition to the time of day, the Mets were ripped by fans and media for making Randolph travel across the country to tell him he was fired, instead of doing it in New York, where he would be returning a day later anyway. "They could've fired Willie Randolph at any point over the last year," comedian and Mets fan Jon Stewart said about the situation during his June 17 broadcast of *The Daily Show*. "Maybe they flew him out to Los Angeles because if we're going to fire him, he should at least get his frequent flier air miles."

8) The Midnight Massacre

After months of disagreements between Tom Seaver and Mets chairman M. Donald Grant about the way the team was spending its money—or not spending its money—Seaver was dealt to the Cincinnati Reds just minutes before the trade deadline in 1977. In return for "Tom Terrific," the face of their franchise, the Mets received Pat Zachry, Doug Flynn, Steve Henderson, and Dan Norman. Moments later, the team also traded away Dave Kingman to the San Diego Padres for Bobby Valentine and Paul Siebert. The Mets finished in last place in five of the next seven years, during which Shea Stadium became known as "Grant's Tomb," an homage to the team's chairman.

9) The Tony Bernazard's shirt scandal

In early 2009 Mets vice president of player development Tony Bernazard visited the organization's Double A affiliate, the Binghamton Mets. According to a July 2009 report by Adam Rubin of the *New York Daily News*, Bernazard spent his visit scolding the team of youngsters after a 1–6 homestand, during which he ripped off his shirt and challenged the minor leaguers to a fight. As a result of the report and ensuing media firestorm, Minaya was forced to fire

Bernazard, who had been his close friend and confidante for several years.

10) Omar Minaya calls out reporter on live TV

In his press conference announcing that Bernazard had been fired, which aired live on SNY, Minaya insinuated that Adam Rubin had an ulterior motive when breaking the story of Bernazard's tantrum in Binghamton. "You gotta understand this: Adam, for the past couple of years, has lobbied for a player development position," Minaya explained, confusing more or less every person watching him speak.

Rubin then asked Minaya if he was alleging that he tried to end Bernazard's career so he could take his job. "No, I'm not saying that," Minaya responded, sitting seemingly scattered and confused in front of a room full of New York reporters. "Adam, you have told me—and you have told other people in the front office—that you want to work for player development in the front office."

Rubin later said Minaya's insinuation and decision to call him out by name was a "low blow" and "despicable." "I thought Omar had a thick skin—obviously not," Rubin said. "They fired Bernazard because he did the things I said he did…For them to change the story like this, personally it devastates me. This is my livelihood…I could assure you they just made my job impossible to do in the short-term."

The confused silence that remained in the media room after these events was palpable. I have no doubt that this was awkward and terrible for everyone involved. But as someone watching from the outside in, it was riveting, totally embarrassing, hilarious, and completely fascinating. In other words, this is without a doubt the most ridiculous, amazingly terrible #LOLMets moment of all time. What's really crazy, though, is that while I mentioned 10 moments above, there are dozens more that easily could have made the list.

Laugh with the Comedians Who Are Mets Fans

Bucket Rank:

In order to be a Mets fan, you have to have a sense of humor. And, in the case of one group of Mets fans, they are known for making people laugh. Chris Rock, Jerry Seinfeld, Jon Stewart, Jimmy Kimmel, and Bill Maher are among the countless, influential, hilariously famous comedians that are also proud, die-hard Mets fans.

In addition to throwing out first pitches and regularly having had Mr. Met on his brilliant, influential late-night show on Comedy Central, *The Daily Show,* Stewart frequently used his broadcast to goof on and encourage his favorite baseball team. During Stewart's final season, he did an entire segment on the surging Mets. Also, earlier in the season, he had Matt Harvey on as a guest. As the two sat down for their interview, Stewart stopped the discussion to put a pillow below Harvey's pitching elbow to make sure it was well protected. Stewart concluded the interview by begging Harvey and the Mets to win a World Series. "You know, I'm leaving the show," Stewart said. "You're all I've got left."

In a two-episode arc during Season Three of *Seinfeld,* Seinfeld essentially dedicated an entire episode to his favorite player, Keith Hernandez, who starred as himself and the love interest of Elaine Benes, the character played by Julia Louis-Dreyfus. It is also revealed later in the episode that characters Kramer and Newman were once spit on by Hernandez after a Mets game at Shea Stadium. In an effort to defend Hernandez from his accusers, Seinfeld leads Kramer and Newman through a parody of the presentation given by Kevin

Costner's character in the film *JFK*. "That was one magic loogie," Seinfeld said, ending his defense, which ultimately put blame on Mets reliever Roger McDowell, not Hernandez. It is also in this episode where Hernandez first uses the saying, "I'm Keith Hernandez," when trying to build up the courage to kiss Benes. The saying was later used by Hernandez during TV ads he did for Just for Men hair coloring products, and it was also the title of his 2017 memoir.

Seinfeld is also known to go on Twitter rants about the team, all of which are right in step with how any other Mets fan would behave during good and bad times. Also like your average fan, he called

Die-hard Mets fan Jerry Seinfeld hangs out with then-Mets manager Jerry Manuel during spring training in 2010. (AP Images)

WFAN anonymously late at night to complain about the team's actions, though was eventually outed and then regularly booked as a guest with host Steve Somers. "I learn something every time I watch it. Sometimes it's about baseball, sometimes it's about life, but it's always something," Seinfeld told ESPN.com. "There is no other game that is so shockingly correct in its original form. You look at the fact that a shortstop bobbles the ball, and the runner can run much faster. It still works out that they still have to do what they do as best as they can and it's still exactly even. That's just incomprehensible. If it's 91 feet, it's different."

Having been raised in River Vale, New Jersey, Maher is such a big Mets fan that he bought a minority share of the team in 2012. "It's a great investment," Maher, who also hosts HBO's *Real Time with Bill Maher,* told local reporters at Citi Field in 2012. "I just thought it would be a great place, especially after I've seen some of the ways money can disappear in recent years. I had my money in Lehman Brothers in 2008."

According to a sale document issued to potential investors, limited partners will be able to get their 2012 investment back with a 3 percent compounded interest as early as 2018.

In an article for *The Wall Street Journal* in 2015, Maher explained that the career path of a comic is very similar to the history of the Mets, which may be part of the reason comedians are drawn to them. "When you're a comic and you start out, you're literally a laughingstock. People aren't laughing with you—they're laughing at you," Maher said. "All of us new comics are humiliated. That is similar to what the Mets were in 1962."

He often talks quite openly about his love of Mets history, especially the teams from the 1960s, which he experienced as a teenager growing up one hour from Shea Stadium. In 1986 he watched the Mets win the World Series with Seinfeld and other comedians at a comedy club in Los Angeles.

TV actor and comedian Kevin James is such a big fan that he required that ABC tape his sitcom, *Kevin Can Wait*, on Long Island as opposed to Los Angeles so he could more frequently take his daughter, Shea, who was named after the Mets' old stadium, and his family to Citi Field to watch the Mets. In an episode of the show, James had Mets right-hander Noah Syndergaard make a guest appearance dressed as Thor during the season's Halloween-themed episode.

In 2015 during the team's 11-game winning streak in April, Jim Breuer started using Facebook to post selfie-style videos from his home within minutes of the game ending. After the Mets completed a sweep toward the end of the winning streak, he filmed himself rummaging through his garage looking for a broom. Born in 1967 on Long Island, Breuer became a Mets fan in 1973. "At first I gravitated to the announcers," he told me in 2015. "I was a little kid, just turning five...My whole street was Mets fans and my whole family."

In the late 1990s when he was a cast member on *Saturday Night Live* and during the height of his fame, Breuer was invited to Yankee Stadium to play in a celebrity softball game. Unfortunately, the game had to be canceled. However, because he was a fan of Breuer from *SNL*, New York Yankees owner George Steinbrenner invited him and comedian Bob Saget to his private suite to watch his team play the Yankees. "We go up, and the whole time I'm thinking, *Yuck, Steinbrenner and the Yankees*, but, still, who ever gets this opportunity?" Breuer said. "He is so passionate about his team. He brought me over to a picture of Thurman Munson, which clearly meant a lot to him, and he was talking about it all so emotionally and getting teary eyed. He's pointing to the field, taking pride in Derek Jeter. And then he turns to me and says, 'You're a big Yankee fan, right?'" Unsure of how to handle the moment, Breuer sheepishly said, "Well, you know, I mean, how do you not root for the Yankees?"

Steinbrenner then asked a photographer to come over and take a picture of himself, Breuer, and Saget for the *New York Post*, who had a reporter in the box covering the event. And, of course, Steinbrenner wanted them all to be wearing Yankees hats. "Oh, man, I'm thinking, *how am I going to do this, how am I going to explain this to all my friends when they see this in the paper?"* Breuer said. "So I held the hat in my hand until the very last second, figuring I'd move it right before the shot, when all of a sudden I hear Steinbrenner say, 'Oh, I should have known you were going to be here,' and he stepped out of the picture to greet mayor Rudy Giuliani, who was entering the room."

Giuliani knew Breuer was a Mets fan because the two had a history of goofing on one another at Yankee Stadium, Shea Stadium, and on the set of *SNL*. In April 1998 at Shea Stadium, Breuer led a large group of Mets fans to boo Giuliani, who had been in the front row on Opening Day. Later that day, Mayor Giuliani told Breuer that he would eventually get his revenge. "*Breuer?* Jim Breuer? Really, George," Giuliani said to Steinbrenner as he entered the suite at Yankee Stadium. "Do you realize he's one of the biggest Yankee haters and he's in *your* suite? He loves the Mets, George, loves them. I'm not even going to tell you the names I've heard him call Derek Jeter."

Steinbrenner turned to Breuer looking stunned and confused. "Is that true, Jim? Is what he's saying true?" he asked in an uncharacteristically soft voice, sounding disappointed and saddened by the news. Thankfully, Giuliani stepped in, smiled, and told Steinbrenner that Breuer was a good guy, loved baseball, and respected the Yankees. Later, as the group watched the Yankees beat the Boston Red Sox, Giuliani leaned in to Breuer and whispered, "I told you I'd get you back one day."

Similar to Breuer, comedian Steve Hofstetter, the host of *Finding Babe Ruth* on FS1 and a former host and executive producer of *Laughs*, grew up a Mets fan because of his family.

He believes comedians gravitate to the Mets because they have an affinity for the underdog.

"There's also an element of anti-establishment," he told me about the mind of a comedian. "And because we're so used to rejection, we're more likely to embrace loss and joke about it."

After researching the topic, the only die-hard, famously funny Yankees fans I came across were Billy Crystal and Larry David. If there is one other team that also has a large following of fans who are also famous comedians, it's the Cubs. For instance, Bill Murray, Vince Vaughn, and Jeff Garlin are routinely spotted at the front row Wrigley Field, getting worked up about balls and strikes just like everyone else. Like Vaughn, two of America's most beloved comedic actors, the late, great Harold Ramis and John Belushi were also Cubs fans. In the two cities with multiple baseball teams (New York and Chicago), comedians must tend to choose the Mets and Cubs, who are known as each town's lovable losers, as concluded in the *WSJ* article.

That may be right. In addition to Seinfeld, Kimmel, Stewart, Maher, Rock, James, Breuer, and Hofstetter, the list of comedian Mets fans also includes Ben Stiller, *Modern Family*'s Ty Burrell, Ray Romano, Amy Schumer, Ed Burns, Matthew Broderick, Richard Kind, and the late and legendary Rodney Dangerfield and George Carlin. There is no franchise in professional sports that has fans this funny.

Get Duped by Sidd Finch

Bucket Rank: 🗑️ 🗑️ 🗑️

In the April 1, 1985, issue of *Sports Illustrated*, sportswriter George Plimpton introduced Sidd Finch, the greatest pitcher in the world, who agreed to a tryout with the Mets a few months earlier. Fans read Plimpton's story and became giddy with excitement to see the young man throw. Reporters at the team's spring training facility eagerly awaited his arrival to camp.

The only problem was that Plimpton invented Finch, the fictitious character and centerpiece of one of the greatest April Fools' Day jokes ever pulled off in sports. *SI*'s managing editor Mark Mulvoy tasked Plimpton with the project a few months earlier after realizing that month's issue's publishing date would fall on April 1. Mulvoy later explained that he wanted a creative, unique writer, who could build a very detailed, fake baseball story to appear at the back of the magazine—given that the publication date would coincide with the start of the season. He immediately thought of Plimpton, who was known for his offbeat, experiential, first-person, participatory journalism, during which he often competed with professional sports teams and then wrote about them from the perspective of a fan.

Plimpton invented Finch, who he said was raised in an English orphanage before moving to Tibet to learn yoga and where he played the French horn. In Tibet he learned to pitch in the snow, wearing one boot on his right foot while his left foot was bare. According to Plimpton, Finch's fastball could hit 168 miles per hour. He had pinpoint control and needed no time to warm up.

Plimpton chose the Mets to be Finch's team.

SI photographer Lane Stewart asked his friend, Joe Benton, to play the role of Finch in the photographs that would be used to accompany Plimpton's story. Berton was a 6'4" middle school art teacher who had no experience playing baseball. The Mets were made aware of the story and allowed Stewart to take photographs of Benton on field with their players in St. Petersburg, Florida, before media arrived to spring training. The Mets also gave Finch a uniform with No. 21 and a locker next to Darryl Strawberry. Mets pitching coach Mel Stottlemyre posed for a picture, pretending to show Finch how to throw a curveball, and hitters looked scared as they watched him throw batting practice. "He's a pitcher, part yogi, and part recluse. Impressively liberated from our opulent life-style, Sidd's deciding about yoga," Plimpton wrote in his lead for the *SI* story.

The first letter of every word—after yogi—spelled out April Fools' Day, but no one noticed.

Mulvoy, Plimpton, Stewart, and Benton did such an incredible job that two Major League Baseball general managers reportedly called the commissioner of Major League Baseball, asking why they were not made aware of Finch's free-agent status. Similarly, competing New York sports editors of daily newspapers complained to the team's public relations director for giving such a big scoop to *Sports Illustrated*. The magazine eventually confessed to the gag once reporters arrived to Mets camp looking for the team's new, amazing, once-in-a-lifetime pitching prospect.

Thankfully, fans, media, baseball executives—and especially scouts—got the joke and the magazine was praised for their outstanding work. In 1987 Plimpton turned the story into a novel titled *The Curious Case of Sidd Finch*, which built on the legend propagated by he and *Sports Illustrated* two years earlier.

It's a funny part of the team's history, even though it isn't a real part of their legacy.

However, it taps in to a belief that Mets fans developed during much of the 1990s and 2000s, which is that all of their prospects may have well been fictitious because so few of them panned out.

Roughly a decade after Plimpton's April Fools' joke, Mets fans were led to believe they had three, real-life versions of Finch, in what was labeled "Generation K." Mets pitching prospects Bill Pulsipher, Jason Isringhausen, and Paul Wilson were highly touted, but they never fulfilled their potential—at least not with the Mets.

The trio made their debut with promise, leading Mets fans to think they were the 1990s answer to Doc Gooden, Sid Fernandez, and Rick Aguilera, collectively talented enough to get the organization back to the World Series. But in time all three pitchers eventually needed Tommy John surgery, a procedure that replaces the ulnar collateral ligament in the pitching elbow and requires at least one year or rehabilitation.

In addition to elbow surgery, Wilson also needed shoulder surgery and spent only the 1996 season with the Mets. He made just 26 starts for the Mets, going 5–12 with a 5.38 ERA before being traded to the Tampa Bay Devil Rays in July of 2000. Isringhausen had three Tommy John surgeries before he retired in 2012, prior to which he was able to put together a 16-year career and collect 300 saves mostly as a respected closer with the St. Louis Cardinals. In 2011, 16 years after making his big league debut in their uniform, he returned to the Mets for whom he played a leadership role in helping mentor the team's young relief pitchers. Pulsipher went 5–9 with a 4.63 ERA in only 20 starts spanning three injury-plagued seasons. He returned from surgery with chronic control issues and was eventually traded to the Milwaukee Brewers in July of 1998. "We had big plans for the future, we believed we were going to be great pitchers," Pulsipher told *Newsday* in 2015, speaking from his home in New York, where he works in road construction. "Things didn't work out the way we had hoped."

The list of overhyped prospects—who fans and executives refused to trade for win-now, proven big league talent, but who never developed to have successful big league careers of their own—is seemingly endless. In the mid-1990s the Mets bragged to reporters that outfield prospect Alex Ochoa was their next great five-tool player and reminiscent of Strawberry. He made his major league debut in late 1995, hit .297 in 37 at-bats, and excited fans for his seemingly unlimited future. However, he hit just four home runs the next season, got pushed to the bench the following year, and was traded to the Minnesota Twins the season after.

Similar to Ochoa, fans were told to get excited about Alex Escobar, a five-tool player who was signed as a non-drafted free agent in 1995. He made his much-anticipated big league debut in 2001, the year after the Mets were in the World Series. He bounced between Triple A and Shea Stadium, appearing in just 18 games. However, he struggled, hitting .200 with three home runs and eight RBIs. Prior to the next season, Escobar was traded to the Cleveland Indians and out of baseball five years later.

In my time writing MetsBlog, no prospect was hyped more than Fernando Martinez. "The Teenage Hitting Machine," as he eventually got labeled, Martinez was rumored to be requested in dozens of trades by general managers all across baseball. However, because he was going to be so good and so important to their future outfield, the Mets would not let him go.

Martinez signed with the Mets at 16 years old in 2005 and made his major league debut four years later. In 91 at-bats he hit just .176 with one home run and eight RBIs before his season ended early due to inflammation in his right knee. He spent the bulk of the following two seasons dealing with similar nagging injuries while appearing in just 18 games. The Mets eventually put him on waivers where he got claimed by the Houston Astros, and he continued to struggle with them. He has not played in the majors since 2013.

Be it Escobar, Ochoa, Martinez, Generation K, or Ryan Thompson, Jason Tyner, Lastings Milledge, Francisco Pena, Ike Davis, Aaron Heilman, Shawn Abner, and Mike Pelfrey, Mets fans have been lead down a bottomless pit of promise when it comes to rising stars. Finch may have been fiction, but the above prospects ended up being fiction, too.

Thankfully, starting in 2012, a robust crop of young, hard-throwing pitchers emerged from the team's farm system and were capable of redeeming the ghosts of prospects past, as well as putting Finch back in his proper comedic place. In 2015 Matt Harvey, Jacob deGrom, Noah Syndergaard, and Steven Matz all helped lead the Mets to their first postseason appearance in nine years. The following season, though, they were all plagued by injury, leading to fear they could end up being another Generation K. However, as of early 2017, the group once again appeared healthy, talented, and ready to bring greatness back to the Mets.

Learn About Davey Johnson and the '86 Mets

Bucket Rank: 🗑️🗑️🗑️🗑️

In spring of 1986, Mets manager Davey Johnson believed in his team the way Mets fans believe in their team. "I lined them up in spring training and told them, 'We're not just gonna win this year; we're going to dominate,'" he explained to me in 2014, recalling the same story he's told countless others about the start of his team's magical 1986 season.

Thankfully for Davey and for Mets fans, he was right. Johnson's 1986 Mets went on to win 108 games in a powerful, arrogant fashion, continuing their success through the postseason and resulting in the organization's second world championship.

In an interesting twist of fate, it was Johnson (then playing for the Baltimore Orioles) who made the final out in 1969, when the Mets won their first World Series. At the time Johnson was in the middle of what would be a 13-year big league career, during which he hit .261 with 136 home runs, while playing for the Orioles, Atlanta Braves, Philadelphia Phillies, and Chicago Cubs. By the time Johnson retired as a player in 1978, he made four All-Star Game appearances and won the Rawlings Gold Glove Award at second base three times. He also won four American League pennants and two World Series championships with the Orioles.

He was hired the next season to be the manager of the Miami Amigos, who played in a pan-Caribbean professional baseball league with no affiliation with Major League Baseball. The league went out of business just 72 games into its only season, after which Johnson went home looking for work in the game he loved.

Finally, in 1981 Johnson was hired to manage the Double A Jackson Mets, who he led to a 68–66 record during his first professional season at the helm. In 1983 Johnson was promoted to manager of the Triple A Tidewater Tides, who finished 71–68. Johnson's 1983 team in Tidewater included Darryl Strawberry, the organization's tall, lanky, 21-year-old first-round draft pick from 1980. Strawberry played just 16 games for Johnson in 1983 before being called up to the Mets, for whom he'd hit 26 home runs, steal 19 bases, and win the National League's Rookie of the Year award. Less than a year later, Johnson and Strawberry would be reunited in Queens.

Managers Frank Howard and then George Bamberger both struggled to lead the Mets in 1983, finishing 68–94 despite a roster that included Strawberry, Tom Seaver, Keith Hernandez, Mookie Wilson, and George Foster. So Johnson got the call to take over the Mets in 1984. In his first season as a big league manager, he won 90 games, which would be the first of five consecutive 90-win seasons.

The 1984 Mets had a talented roster, which was propelled in large part by 19-year-old Dwight Gooden, who was promoted from Single A to make the Opening Day roster. Gooden captivated baseball from his first pitch, immediately establishing himself as one of the league's most talented pitchers. In 1984 under the leadership of Johnson and with just one season of professional baseball under his belt, Gooden made the All-Star team, won the National League's Rookie of the Year award, and led the league in strikeouts. In 1985 he would win the National League's Cy Young Award with a league-leading 24 wins, 1.53 ERA, and 268 strikeouts. He also had 16 complete games.

Prior to 1985, the Mets traded for seven-time All-Star catcher Gary Carter, who, along with Hernandez, provided Johnson two veteran leaders who would help shape the team's attitude and character on and off the field. It would be only a few months later at the organization's spring training home in Al Lang Stadium in St. Petersburg, Florida, that Johnson would tell his team they were going to dominate baseball and win a World Series. "We won 95 games in 1985 and still got beat by the Cardinals. But the next offseason, we added Bob Ojeda, Tim Teufel, and Ray Knight and—right then, right there—I knew there'd be nothing Cardinals manager Whitey Herzog could do to match us," Johnson told me in 2014, when I asked him why he was so confident heading in to 1986. "I truly believed in our talent. I knew there was no way St. Louis was gonna take us."

It may have also helped that Johnson was one of the first baseball managers to use computers and statistics to better prepare himself, his staff, and his players for games. Thanks in large part to his degree in mathematics from Trinity University, Johnson told *PC Magazine* in 1984 that, while playing for the Orioles, he frequently used their IBM 360 mainframe to develop models that projected likely outcomes for in-game situations. He also said that he may have been the first person to discover the importance of on-base percentage, which measures how often a batter reaches base. "It makes sense that if you bat the players in the order of the highest on-base percentage and all the way down, obviously you'd get more guys to come up to the plate," he said. "The more guys you can get up to the plate, the better chance you have to score runs."

He told *The New York Times* in 1985 that on-base percentage was the basis for him replacing Mookie Wilson in the leadoff spot of his batting order with Wally Backman. "[The computer] tells you what may happen, so that you can make things come out more favorably," Johnson told *The Times* 20 years before A's general manager Billy Beane popularized statistical analysis in baseball.

As he predicted, Johnson's 1986 Mets went on to dominate, winning a franchise-record 108 games and the National League East. They defeated the Houston Astros in six games in the National League Championship Series and beat the American League champion Boston Red Sox in seven games to win the World Series.

However, the season wasn't all winning and celebrating. In July four Mets players were arrested after an early morning altercation with two police officers at a bar in Houston. Teufel, Ron Darling, Ojeda, and Rick Aguilera spent 11 hours in a holding cell before being released on bail in time for the next day's game. In general, the team's partying and drug abuse has become notorious. Their hard-partying ways have been written about in books, covered in films, and talked about by fans for decades. Wrote The Daily Beast: "The bulk of the team drank to excess after every game, win or lose, chased women like it was written into their contracts, and got into brawls both on and off the field spurred by a quick-trigger rage to rival soccer hooligans."

In his book *Game 7, 1986: Failure and Triumph in the Biggest Game of My Life*, Darling writes poetically about how his teammates relied on a mix of pregame amphetamines and late-game beers to power themselves through aches, pains, hangovers, and a 162-game season.

"You'd see guys toward the end of a game, maybe getting ready for their final at-bat, double-back into the locker room to chug a beer...so they could step to the plate completely wired and focused and dialed in," he wrote. "They had it down to a science with precision timing... They'd get this rush of confidence that was through the roof and step to the plate like the world-beaters they were born to be."

The night the Mets defeated the Astros during the NLCS, the players and their wives partied so aggressively on a flight back to New York they caused $7,500 damage to the airplane. "When we walked off that plane I was like, 'Oh, my god, this is insane.' We tore up the whole plane,'" Strawberry detailed during a 2016 online documentary about the incident for *Victory Journal*.

Appalled by the team's behavior, Mets GM Frank Cashen tried to get Johnson and his players to pay the $7,500 bill for the airplane, according to multiple reports. However, Johnson crumbled up the paper in front of his players, threw it at Cashen, and said, "We just won you the f--king pennant, you pay for it," the team's third baseman Kevin Mitchell relayed to Victory Journal.

This was only the beginning, as tension and disagreements between Johnson and the team's front office continued to escalate. In time Cashen made several personnel moves that Johnson did not agree with, which, in the manager's view, systematically weakened the team, resulting in less and less success during the late '80s. In late May of 1990, with the Mets 20–22, Cashen fired Johnson despite the Mets finishing 87–75 and in second place the year before. "I felt our ballclub was underachieving," Cashen told reporters at the time of Johnson's dismissal. "The time came to head in a new direction. I talked to the team about underachieving and having fire in the belly. I want this team to focus on winning because winning is what it is all about."

In talking with Johnson in 2014, I got the impression that he was proud of how confident and eccentric his team was in 1986 but also slightly embarrassed that they may now be more remembered for the partying than their success on the field. In either case he is clearly proud of how he handled them and for having led them to the winner's circle. "I treated them like men," he told me, noting that to gain their trust it was important to always show respect for them as people, not just ballplayers. "As long as they won and played the game right, I didn't care what they were doing in the clubhouse or after the game."

In the end Johnson won 595 games for the Mets, including a world championship. He never finished worse than second place. Despite just seven seasons, he is still their winningest manager, and his 1,012 games at the helm are the most in team history. "He played the game and really understood what the clubhouse was supposed to be like," Strawberry told SI Now. "He just let us be loose. He let us be ourselves. He didn't allow the front office to make decisions about what was going on in the clubhouse. Davey ran the clubhouse the way he wanted to run it and he just allowed us to be players and have fun. It was just incredible. I mean, we were crazy. It was like *Animal House*. But when we stepped between the lines, it was all business."

After the Mets, Johnson went on to manage the Reds, Orioles, Los Angeles Dodgers, and Washington Nationals, making the postseason with each organization but the Dodgers. Among managers with at least 1,000 games managed, he currently ranks 13th with a .562 winning percentage. He is one of only seven managers in baseball history to win Manager of the Year in both leagues. But to Mets fans, he'll always be remembered as the man in the blue satin Mets jacket, peering toward the field while leaning on a bent knee from the top of the dugout steps in Shea Stadium.

Understand Why Hodges Belongs in the Hall of Fame

Bucket Rank: 🗑️🗑️🗑️🗑️🗑️

The Mets drafted first baseman Gil Hodges in the 1961 Expansion Draft. He was 37 years old and several years beyond his prime. However, he held a special place in New York's heart for his accomplishments as a power-hitting, eight-time All-Star with the Brooklyn Dodgers.

Hodges left for Los Angeles when the team moved west in 1958. So, his return to New York baseball was viewed as a nostalgic homecoming and perfectly timed for the end of his career.

He proudly took the field with the Mets during their inaugural season and then retired as a player in early May after playing just 11 games the following year. He was immediately hired to manage the

Washington Senators, who were coming off back-to-back 100-loss seasons.

After Casey Stengel retired as manager of the Mets, the team went a combined 146–244 under Wes Westrum and Salty Parker. With a crop of young players coming to the big leagues, including Tom Seaver, it was time for the Mets to hire a new leader.

In five years at the helm in Washington, Hodges never finished with a winning record. However, his team improved its play and won more games each season he was in charge. Hodges' Senators eventually climbed from the bottom to finish in sixth place in the 10-team American League, making him the perfect choice to lead the Mets in 1968. The Mets traded $100,000 and pitcher Bill Denehy to get Hodges from the Senators. And in his first year back in New York, this time as their manager, he led the Mets to 73 wins. At the time it was their most successful season in franchise history, giving the organization and their fans hope entering his second year in command.

Hodges' Mets played subpar baseball through the first two months of 1969. Thankfully, an 11-game winning streak got them back on their feet. Of course, it was hardly noticed within the National League since Leo Durocher's Chicago Cubs with Ferguson Jenkins, Ron Santo, and Ernie Banks were capturing baseball's hearts and minds while looking to win their first World Series title in 61 years. By mid-August, with six weeks left in the season, the Cubs held a nine-and-a-half-game lead on the Mets, which they seemed unlikely to lose. Hodges and his Mets had a different plan, though, as they won 38 of their final 49 games. In the midst of their second 10-game winning streak of the season, two of which were against Chicago, the Mets surpassed the free-falling Cubs in the standings during early September and never looked back.

In the end Hodges won 100 games and did it mostly by platooning players in and out of a variety of positions. He ended with 11 men on his roster each of whom appeared in at least 100 games. Outfielders Cleon Jones and Tommie Agee were the only players on his team to get more than 400 at-bats. His mixing and matching of Ron Swoboda and Art Shamsky gave him 23 home runs and 99 RBIs out of right field, while Ed Kranepool and Donn Clendenon combined to hit 23 more home runs and 86 RBIs at first base.

Hodges' Mets then defeated the Atlanta Braves in the National League Championship Series. Like the Mets, the Braves were a very hot team at the end the regular season, winning 17 of their final 21 games. However, New York hit an impressive .327 with six home runs to sweep the series in three games.

Just as they had been to start the season, as well as at the beginning of the NLCS, the Mets took the field as underdogs against the American League champion Baltimore Orioles. Thanks in part to Don Buford's first-inning home run against Tom Seaver, the Orioles won the first game of the series, further making a Mets championship feel like an impossibility. However, from that point forward, Hodges' pitching staff dominated Baltimore's potent offense, holding them to just a .146 average during the series. The Mets had been the laughingstock of baseball for much of the 1960s, so no one expected them to finish near first place in 1969, let alone win the World Series. However, in the same year the United States first put a man on the moon, the Mets reached their ultimate goal, defeating the Orioles in five games.

Hodges' 1969 Mets are now often referred to as "the Miracle Mets" because of how their World Series victory left America and the baseball world in stunned disbelief. However, Seaver told me in 2007 that he never liked that term because he felt it made Hodges and his teammates appear only lucky. In his mind, they knew entering 1969 that they had a chance to win a world championship, and it was everyone else in baseball that was unaware of their potential. "We knew we were a good team," he told me while still seeming offended more than 30 years later. "We knew we had great pitching and a great leader in Gil Hodges. So, we were not surprised by what we accomplished. Understand, Gil got us to believe this was what we were supposed to do, which is the hallmark of a real leader. Was it a shock to baseball and New York? I suppose so because it turned everyone upside down."

Sadly, Hodges passed away of a heart attack prior to the start of the 1972 season. He was just 47 years old. Despite only managing the Mets for four seasons, Hodges is a legendary figure in team history. He was immortalized the year after he died by becoming one of only four Mets to have his number retired.

In 2007 I asked Seaver to describe Hodges as a manager. Seaver is always serious and deliberate when he speaks—be it about baseball, wine, or the weather. He rarely smiles. However, any time I've ever discussed with or heard him talk about Hodges, he gets more focused and becomes passionate in a way he doesn't when speaking about other topics. "He was important to the Brooklyn Dodgers, he played a major role in getting Jackie Robinson to the big leagues, which is one of the best things to ever happen in baseball," Seaver told me. "When you combine that with his time playing and managing, his ability to hit in that lineup, not to mention his character and the way he honored and respected the game, he very much deserves to be in the Hall of Fame."

It's clear that Seaver loved Hodges like a father and—given how highly regarded Seaver is among Mets fans—it's understandable that this respect and appreciation is similarly felt in the stands. However, Hodges is not in the Major League Baseball Hall of Fame, much to the bewilderment of Seaver and his teammates, as well as countless Mets and Dodgers fans. It's an odd outcome given that he's one of the few people in baseball to have success as a player and manager.

In addition to winning 660 games in nine seasons as a manager, including a World Series for the Mets in 1969, he was also an integral part of the 1940s and 1950s Dodgers, winning seven National League pennants and two World Series. In his 18-year career, he hit .273, 370 home runs, 1,274 RBIs, 1,921 hits and he scored 1,105 runs. He made the All-Star team eight times, won three Gold Gloves, and finished in the top 10 in MVP voting three times. During his prime from 1951 to 1957, he averaged 33 home runs and 106 RBIs each season while continuing to be a stellar fielder at first base. When Hodges retired as a player in 1967, he ranked 11th on baseball's all-time home run list. The 10 players ahead of him are all in the Hall of Fame, while Hodges is not.

Hodges failed to make the Hall of Fame during all 15 years that he was eligible. He first appeared on the Veterans Committee ballot in 1987, but he still never received the 75 percent of votes needed for entry. Similarly, he's been unable to receive the necessary amount of votes from the Golden Era Committee, though he'll continue being eligible for consideration every three years. "Every year I hope that Gil earns what I feel is his proper spot in Cooperstown and thus far I've been disappointed," my friend, Brian Erni, wrote for SNY.TV in 2014. "What he was able to accomplish in 1969 remains one of the most stunning miracles in sports. Add to that his imposing offensive presence on the great Dodgers teams of the '50s, and I think his resume speaks for itself."

In the aftermath of his death, the Associated Press published a series of quotes from Hodges' contemporaries—Durocher, Stengel, Robinson, Johnny Podres, Duke Snider, and Seaver, all of whom praised his character and passion for the game. "He was the most important man in my career," Seaver told me, which was followed by a long silence, as if he wanted me to think extra hard about what that statement meant to him. "He was tough. He was a true foxhole guy and the embodiment of strength. Not everybody liked him, but we all respected him. He was serious about his job and a true professional and he inspired me to go about my job in the same way."

Learn About the Other Mr. Met

Bucket Rank: 🗑 🗑 🗑 🗑 🗑

David Wright made his big league debut with the Mets on July 21, 2004, in front of a sparse crowd at Shea Stadium. The Mets won just 71 games that season, finishing in fourth place in the National League East. However, more than two years later and just 383 games in to his career, Wright would be starting at third base for the Mets in the National League Championship Series, getting as far as one game away from the World Series.

Sadly, he would not get back to playing postseason baseball for another nine seasons. In between, Wright collected 1,312 hits, hit .296 with 168 home runs, and made the All-Star Game six times. More importantly, he became the team's leader, the official captain, the player fans identified with, and the main guy the media always turned to for answers. In short, he was the face of the franchise while battling injuries, weak rosters, losing seasons, rebuilds, questions about ownership, fan frustration, and always handling it with aplomb.

In November of 2012, after 1,262 games in a Mets uniform, Wright became a free agent, giving him the opportunity to leave the Mets for a new organization, perhaps one with less attention, less pressure, and a better chance to win. Instead, despite four consecutive losing seasons and a new front office working to reimagine the franchise, Wright signed an eight-year, $138 million contract to remain with the Mets through 2020. "I've grown up in this organization and made lifelong friendships with teammates, uniform personnel, and front-office staff," Wright said when the deal was announced. "I'm grateful

Third baseman David Wright, who has been with the Mets since 2004, is the face of the franchise. (AP Images)

for the opportunity to finish what I've started and help bring the Mets and our fans a World Series title."

In 2015 Wright returned from an early-season injury to again take the field for the Mets in the postseason. The Mets would eventually lose to the Kansas City Royals in the World Series. The unique moment was not wasted on Wright, who grew up a Mets fan in Virginia, living a few miles from the team's Triple A affiliate in Norfolk. "The coolest thing for me was getting a chance to veer off into the crowd during the World Series and see the joy on the faces of Mets fans, all of which had our backs for so long and now were finally getting a chance to come to Citi Field to see a World Series game," Wright told me. "It was one of the most satisfying feelings of my career."

Matthew Cerrone: "What do you remember from the morning of your first day at Shea Stadium?"

David Wright: "Well, that's actually funny because that morning I woke up in Virginia—in my hometown—because I was playing for the Norfolk Tides, and I don't even think I slept the night before because I was told by our manager, John Stearns, that I was going to the big leagues later that night. So, the friends I grew up with and I celebrated a little and then I celebrated with my parents and family that lived there and by the time I got packed up and in bed, it couldn't have been before 2:00, 3:00 AM, and I had to catch a flight first thing the next morning. So my first morning I woke up in Virginia with an incredible amount of adrenalin, getting on an hour-long flight and going straight to the field, where I spent the first couple of hours sitting in my locker staring at my jersey."

MC: "What do you remember about your first big-league at-bat?"

David Wright: "All I wanted to do was look at the scoreboard with my face on it. I'll never forget it. I was walking to the plate, trying to be cool and soak it all in that this is my first major league at-bat—and all I kept doing was looking up at the scoreboard and looking at myself in a Mets uniform on the Jumbotron, the same Jumbotron I was trying to hit during batting practice when I was 18 years old and first signed."

MC: "Do you appreciate how unique it is to be a Major League Baseball player?"

David Wright: "I've been so lucky. And I think I've been told this so many times by family. My father was a police officer, my mom worked in the school system, I have a brother that's an engineer, another brother that is a business major, my youngest brother is about to graduate college. And on a consistent basis they tell me how lucky I am to play baseball for a living. So I think it really hits home. I don't know what my life would be like without baseball.

Sure, there are some days when it's a rough day at the office. But you look back on it, and I think, *I get to play baseball for a living.* And I remember being a kid going out to games and yelling and screaming for autographs and telling my dad how cool it was that these guys got to pay baseball every day and so I try to remember that as often as possible. There's a kid out there in the stands that's watching me for the first time, and I'm going to do whatever I can to play the game the way I think it's meant to be played, have fun, enjoy it, and play hard because this kid could look at me and say to himself, 'I'd like to grow up to be the next Mets third basemen,' and I don't want to let him down when he comes to the games and watches me for the first time.

"I literally grew up with my dad telling me—not in a negative way—that chances are I was never going to play baseball for a living. I've had elementary school teachers that have come up to me or my parents and given me papers and stories from me as a kid saying, 'I'm going to play Major League Baseball.' And the teachers were like, 'Yeah, yeah, yeah, I'm sure you will.' My parents were the same way, saying, 'You need to get your education.' To this day my dad is harping on me because, when I'm done with baseball, he wants me to go back to school and get a college degree. There's not one time where I visit my parents that does not get brought up, and he is trying to convince me that this is the way to go.

"That type of upbringing certainly gives you an outlook and a foundation where I hope I never become the salty, bitter kind of older guy. I want to always view the game like Saturday mornings when I played Little League. It's why I can't wait to get to the field and spend all day there just watching baseball, playing baseball, practicing baseball because that's how much I treasure this game and how much respect and joy I have for it and what it's been able to do for my life. Baseball has given me so much more than I could have ever dreamed. Getting the chance to call Citi Field and Shea Stadium my office is about as cool as it gets."

MC: "What have you learned about Mets fans during your 13-year career?"

David Wright: "The loyalty that this fanbase has shown me personally has been off the charts and something that—when it's all said and done—I think that mutual respect is the biggest thing for me. It's not just about coming to the ballpark and watching a baseball game for Mets fans. They know the game. They know when you do something well that may not show up in the box score. And they know when you didn't get the job done. They don't just come to the ballpark, watch a game, have a beer, have a hot dog, go home, and don't think about it anymore. I mean, it just seems like our fanbase is a lot more rabid. The knowledge level is so high, the expectations are always so high, and I think that makes it a lot more fun to come to the ballpark when fans appreciate you hitting a ground ball to the second basemen with a guy on second and nobody out and getting a runner to third. I think there's more of an appreciation for that than other places when you do the small things correctly."

MC: "Why do you think that is?"

David Wright: "I think a lot of fans that I encounter on the streets in a casual setting grew up playing baseball. In New York, for whatever reason, it seems like everybody's played baseball, whether it was an older guy that played stickball in Brooklyn, a younger guy that played or is playing college or high school baseball or adult league baseball.

It doesn't matter what level; it could be Wiffle Ball. I just think they just love talking about the game. They love interacting and talking shop. It's not just, 'Hey, nice win last night.' For instance, when I'm struggling at the plate, I suddenly meet thousands of hitting coaches when I'm walking down the street to get a sandwich in New York. And that's a good thing. That's cool because they're into the game. It's more than just wins and losses. They want to get to know you as a person and as a player. They want to offer advice. It's cool that there's that type of intensity where you can get stopped on the street, and they feel like they can genuinely help you out because they played high school baseball or they went to fantasy camp last year or they've been watching you since you were 18 years old. That's awesome. That speaks to that passion and that intensity there is for baseball in New York."

Chapter 2

Things to Do

Believe!

Bucket Rank: 🗑️ 🗑️ 🗑️ 🗑️ 🗑️

"**Y**a Gotta Believe" is more than a mantra; it is a string of words that set a tone for a franchise. It slowly became an identity and rallying cry for the Mets and their fans. It nearly died a decade ago at Shea Stadium but found new life at Citi Field in 2015.

Entering the 1973 season, the Mets were a heavy favorite to win their National League divison. However, due to a series of significant injuries, they dropped to 11½ games back of first place by the middle of August. Later that month, given their experience in 1969, Mets chairman of the Board M. Donald Grant addressed the team and told them to keep fighting and that they had the talent to make up ground and win the National League. Mets reliever Tug McGraw reportedly stood up and shouted, "That's right, we can do it, Ya Gotta Believe."

The Yogi Berra-led Mets went on to win 24 of their final 35 games to move into first place on September 21. McGraw's friend, Joe Badamo, who was a motivational speaker, planted the mantra in the relief pitcher's mind a month earlier, MLB.com's Marty Noble wrote in 2015. According to Noble, McGraw had been muttering the mantra to himself and teammates through much of July and the weeks before Grant's meeting with players.

During Grant's speech, Noble said McGraw not only yelled, "Ya Gotta Believe," but also followed it up by prancing around the clubhouse, repeating it over and over again like a war chant.

This is also around the time Berra birthed the saying, "It ain't over 'til it's over," though many believe he was referring to a specific game in July, not the overall pennant race.

In time McGraw's teammates bought in and began repeating the phrase, saying, "Ya Gotta Believe," to fans, reporters, one another, and opponents—to the point that it went from rallying cry to slogan. On October 1, the final game of the regular season, the Mets beat the Chicago Cubs 6–4 at Wrigley Field to win their division. McGraw, who pitched three scoreless innings in relief of Tom Seaver to end the game, had a 1.03 ERA during the last five weeks of the regular season.

In the National League Championship Series, the Mets faced the Cincinnati Reds, who won had 17 more games than New York. The series is most famous for a fight between Reds infielder Peter Rose and Mets infielder Bud Harrelson. With the series tied 1–1, Harrelson was met at second base by a hard-sliding Pete Rose during the fifth inning of Game 3. The two began pushing and shoving, which quickly escalated into an all-out brawl. The two teams left their bullpens and benches to clutter the field with brawling players, while angry Mets fans started throwing napkins and cups on the grass. In the end the Mets won the game 9–2 to take a 2–1 lead in the best-of-five series.

The Reds won Game 4 in Cincinnati, pushing the deciding Game 5 to Shea Stadium.

The Mets held a 7–2 lead in the ninth inning. Seaver got one out but loaded the bases, at which point Berra decided to bring in McGraw. He got Joe Morgan to pop out, which was followed by a game-ending ground-out. Despite being 12 games back in the middle of August, the Mets were heading to the World Series. Their fans stormed the field as the Shea Stadium scoreboard read: "Guess who's 1973 National League Champion? Would you believe the NY Mets. Well you better believe."

Unfortunately, despite being up 3–2 after five games, the Mets lost the World Series in seven games to Reggie Jackson's Oakland A's, who entered as heavy favorites to take the title.

The 1973 Mets may not be looked upon in the same way as the 1969 or 1986 teams—or even the 2000 team that lost to the New York

Yankees. However, when you hear a Mets fan raise a sign, wear a shirt, or scream, "Ya Gotta Believe," it's proof that McGraw's mantra and legacy live on.

"Ya Gotta Believe" was less prevalent in 1986 because the team was such a heavy favorite and dominated the regular season. It crept up again, though, among some fans at Shea Stadium during the late 1990s, when the Mets were viewed as more of an underdog.

Tug McGraw, who coined the mantra "Ya Gotta Believe" gives a thumbs up after saving Game 5 of the 1973 World Series. (AP Images)

And it had a rebirth in 2006, when the organization embraced it again as part of its marketing materials. It also helped that the Mets dominated the National League East and advanced to the NLCS after a fast organizational rebuild that started just two years earlier.

Unfortunately, the Mets lost the 2006 National League Championship Series to the St. Louis Cardinals in a roller coaster Game 7. It was a crushing loss because most experts, media, and fans predicted the Mets would win and face the Detroit Tigers in the World Series. New York had momentum and energy after a brilliant catch by Endy Chavez that robbed a home run, saved the season, and gave the Mets new life. But Cardinals pitcher Adam Wainwright paralyzed Carlos Beltran and stunned Mets fans with his legendary, mind-boggling curveball that dropped in for a called strike three to end the game and send St. Louis to the World Series.

The Mets and their fans began 2007 believing that, while 2006 was disappointing and painful, it was a natural progression in the rebuilding process. The franchise was set back after losing to the Yankees in the 2000 World Series, after which they stripped down, changed personnel, and started a new climb to the top. In 2006 they got to the NLCS. It was assumed in 2007 they would advance to the World Series. It was all part of the plan...until the Philadelphia Phillies came along.

The Mets were enjoying a smooth season as expected, sitting in first place with a seven-game lead and only 17 games to play in the season. It was the last time I ever posted the Magic Number on MetsBlog.com because from that point forward the Mets began a slide in the standings no one ever believed was possible.

The Phillies entered play September 13, having won just four of their previous 11 games. They were reeling. The Mets, on the other hand, had won nine of their previous 11 and were steamrolling like they did the season before. The two teams then met for three games at Shea Stadium, during which they seemingly switched uniforms. The Phillies won all three games as well as nine of their last 13, while the

Mets did the opposite, falling into a tailspin that included a five-game losing streak during the final week of the season.

The two teams took the field tied for first place on the final game of the year. With a New York win, the worst that could happen would be a head-to-head tiebreaker in the event both teams finished the regular season with the same record. In other words, despite all of the chaos and stress and madness from the previous two weeks the Mets still could have reached the postseason by simply beating the Florida Marlins on the last day of the season. But before some Mets fans could even get off the train and find their seats, Tom Glavine had given up seven runs in the top of the first inning.

Mets players, coaches, and fans were left with nothing to do but stare at the out-of-town scoreboard in hopes that the Washington Nationals would do the same to the Phillies. But there would be no such luck, as Philadelphia won easily 6–1 to win the NL East crown and boot the Mets from playoff contention all while completing one of the most amazing comeback stories in baseball history.

In my 13 years writing MetsBlog.com and an entire lifetime spent as a Mets fan, I've never experienced that level of Groundhog Day-like paralysis that we all suffered through in 2007. The fans had the same look on their faces as the players, who had the same look as the manager, who had the same look as the media, who had the same look as the fans. We were all going through it together, though playing different roles in the story. The season went from being a cakewalk to utter nightmare within a week. In a matter of days, it felt like we were all frozen, falling out of an airplane, waiting for someone to spring a parachute that would eventually never open. Understandably, everyone involved with the Mets entered 2008 in a downbeat, wary, delicate state of mind.

The two previous seasons had ended in such dramatic, painful unbelievable ways—both of which were counter to how we viewed the franchise as well as our history as fans and as a franchise—that our faith in "Ya Gotta Believe," "Miracles," and the "Amazin Mets," was starting to buckle. Yet again, just like the season before, the Mets were in first place during the middle of September. However, by the time the team returned home for the final seven games ever at Shea Stadium, the Phillies had taken back first place and moved the Mets in to second. Thankfully, with the clock ticking and seven games to go, the Mets held a one-and-a-half-game lead over the Milwaukee Brewers for the only available wild-card spot. But sadly, during the next five days, the Mets would split with the Cubs, and the Brewers would sweep to also move ahead of the Mets.

For the second year in a row, the Mets season would come down to the final day of the year, but this time it had the potential to also be the final game ever played in Shea Stadium. In the event the Mets advanced to the postseason, they would have the opportunity for a few more home games. However, a loss would shut the door forever.

By mid afternoon, though, the outcome no longer mattered. The Brewers defeated the Cubs to win the wild-card before the Mets even finished playing their game against the Marlins. I've never heard Shea Stadium so quiet and seen fans looking so melancholy and bewildered, contemplating in deep thought whether to go home or stay and watch the already-scheduled postgame celebration honoring Shea Stadium.

The tribute was wonderful and well orchestrated. It was a lovely, sentimental good-bye to our home of 45 years, and yet nobody seemed to care. Sitting there, watching every notable person from the franchise's history be paraded to home plate, I found myself occasionally glancing up at the scoreboard as if it would change. But, nope, the Mets still lost, and the Brewers still won. *Hey, look, Jerry Koosman, Willie Mays, and Yogi Berra.* The Mets still lost, and the Brewers still won. *Wow, Mike Piazza and Tom Seaver are together in the same place.* Ugh, the Mets still lost, and the Brewers still won.

The weight of the day, the losing, the second collapse in two years, and knowing we would never see another game again in Shea Stadium was all so much to digest at the time. As a franchise the

Mets always seemed to find a miracle when they needed it. They found one in 1969, in 1973, 1986, 1999, and 2000. The Mets were the guys who everyone doubted but shocked baseball by benefitting from unbelievable moments. The difference in 2006, 2007, and 2008, though, was that the Mets held the advantage, were the favorites, and still blew the lead. It was the other teams that found the miracle. And the worst part is that it all happened inside the building we loved, which was about to be destroyed. It was surreal.

In 2012, with the Mets now playing in Citi Field, they found themselves in first place during early June, and I recall writing "Ya Gotta Believe" to my thousands of followers on Twitter. However, despite being an expected, somewhat miraculous 31–23, fans sarcastically replied, "Ya Gotta Bereave." Sure enough, the Mets lost 52 of their final 83 games and ended the season miles away from October. I started to hear that the franchise's "Ya Gotta Believe" spirit died with Shea Stadium.

The Mets entered 2015 expecting to be better than their 79 wins the season before. In fact, they spent the entire winter and all of spring training telling reporters how they would be a playoff team. Nevertheless, of the 15 published experts at ESPN.com, all picked the Nationals to win the NL East, and none had the Mets in the playoffs. The same can be said for SI.com, MLB.com, and CBS Sports. MLB reporter Jon Heyman was literally the only one on those sites to give the Mets an outside chance at the wild-card. "Ya Gotta Believe, right?" Mets outfielder Michael Cuddyer said on April 14 with the Mets just 4–3 to start the season. "You've got to believe you're a good team."

According to Terry Collins, "Ya Gotta Believe" returned in spring training before the season even started and explained Cuddyer's use of the mantra. "We had a couple of meetings in spring training, where different guys stood up, that they never did in the past, and said: 'Listen, we're good enough,'"Collins told reporters. "Cuddyer said it, David said it, Curtis Granderson said it...You start to pay attention because, hey, these guys believe, and if the stars believe, if you're a young player, you better believe in yourself and you better believe that we can get this done."

The Mets continued winning through April, taking 11 straight games at one point, ending the month 15–8 and in first place by four and a half games over the Nationals. "I don't think I meant for it to be a catchphrase," Cuddyer admitted to me in late 2016. "For me, I just felt that our team [in 2015] was good and full of winners. Because the team and organization hadn't won in a long time, I just wanted to get the message across that they had to believe they were winners—and believe that they had what it took to win. It was about truly changing the mind-set rather than just a catchphrase for people to start saying."

The Mets had an eight and a half game lead in the NL East with 17 games to play on September 15, 2015. However, because of what happened with 17 games left eight years earlier, I wrote this that day on MetsBlog.com: "It's officially September, the Mets are in first place, and I'm nervous...Like it or not, the nightmare of 2007 and 2008 is baked into my experience as a Mets fan. I know it's irrational, since one situation has nothing to do with the other...I know I should ignore memories of Willie Randolph talking about champagne, Tom Glavine's seven-run fiasco and so on. I pride myself on being a 'Ya Gotta Believe' type of guy. I grew up on miracles. It's not like I want to be paranoid. I'd rather look at the standings, see the Nationals meandering, see the Mets winning, and be overly confident, chest out, eyes wide open, and enjoy the show. But I can't. I just can't do it, at least not until the ghosts of 2007 and 2008 (and Carlos Beltran's NLCS strikeout in 2006) are beaten out of my reality. So, please 2015, help me out here, go full steam, don't let up, and don't look back...so I can start looking forward and believe again."

The Mets eventually won the NL East in 2015, defeated the Los Angeles Dodgers and Cubs in the postseason and got to their first World Series since 2000, much to the surprise of literally every expert in baseball. Of course, just like Seaver's Mets in 1969, the Mets always believed they could do it. I'm sorry to say most fans were skeptical and a nervous wreck right up until the end, myself included. Despite the season ending in a loss to the Kansas City Royals, 2015 marked the revival of the franchise as well as an important mantra that Mets fans hold dear to their hearts. Again, we believe...

. . . .

Cheer with Cowbell Man

Bucket Rank:

If you close your eyes during a game at Citi Field and listen closely, you'll hear him.

It may be faint and far in the distance, but you'll hear it.

Tonk! Tonk! Tonk!

Tonk! Tonk! Tonk!

His name is Eddie Boison. But to Mets fans, he is "Cowbell Man."

In 1995 at Shea Stadium, Boison hit his cowbell during a game for the first time. And a legend was born. "I used to play in a Latin band and I brought a cowbell to a game at Shea to do some practice," Boison told Matt Silverman in the 2012 book, *Best Mets*. "DiamondVision put up 'Let's Go Mets,' and I started playing along with their rendition. Then people started to applaud. I brought the cowbell back to another game and saw that people were responding."

Today, he goes to his section in Citi Field wearing a Mets hat, a big smile, and an authentic blue jersey with No. 21 that reads, "Cowbellman," across the back. Personally, I prefer Boison's black and blue batting practice jersey that he rocked at Shea, which read, "Cowbell Man."

Boison, who is in his late 50s, will only miss a game for family emergencies. At first, he only regularly attended games at Shea Stadium on Tuesday and Friday, as part of a trial season-ticket package. Eventually, he started buying single tickets before each game. He now has a full, 81-game ticket plan, which he pays for out of his own pocket.

The first time I met Eddie was—oddly enough—at Yankee Stadium. My wife is a die-hard New York Yankees fan. As part of a segment about our inter-rival marriage, SNY sent me and her to a regular-season Subway Series game two days before our wedding.

Tonk! Tonk! Tonk!

Tonk! Tonk! Tonk!

"Wait, is that Cowbell Man?" I said, stopping my then-fiancee before entering the stadium.

Eddie and I talked for a minute. Then, I asked if I could start a "Let's Go Mets" chant with his cowbell. He allowed it. And I'm not going to lie, I felt special and awesome. It turns out I wasn't that special at all. If asked nicely, Boison routinely allows fans to use his instrument. "Hit it right in the middle," he told Silverman about the best way to strike a cowbell.

"People think you have to hit it hard. Just tap it, and the sound takes care of itself."

Shea Stadium was more conducive than Citi Field to Cowbell Man's talents because he could walk around each section with total freedom. In Citi Field, he says, there are a lot more stairs and exclusive sections that break up access to certain parts of the ballpark. It doesn't matter, though, because you still hear him. He may be on the porch over right field, hanging with fans on the Shea Bridge or walking behind you on the Promenade, but he's always there.

Tonk! Tonk! Tonk!

Tonk! Tonk! Tonk!

In addition to Cowbell Man, be on the lookout for Pin Man, Tie Guy, and Vernon the Fireman Koooler, who are also staples at Citi Field. Pin Man, whose real name is Nick Giampietro, wears a white, pinstriped Mets jersey that has more than 200 pins on it. Of course, on the back he has the name, "Pin Man." His jersey doesn't have a number so that he has more room for pins.

Like Boison, Giampietro has season tickets and comes to every home game. The pins are special, as they each mark a signature moment from the team's entire history. However, I'm most impressed with his hat, which has flashing pins and an LED sign that scrolls between "Let's Go Mets!" and "Mets Win!" If you see Nick, stop and talk with him. He's super nice, always smiling, and more than happy to talk to anyone about his collection.

It's okay to say hello to Vernon, too, even though he watches the game with an intense glare. Gibson, also known as Fireman Koooler, is a former volunteer fireman, who watches every game perched on a railing along the Shea Bridge, where he is focused squarely on the action at hand. You can't miss him because he'll be wearing reflective sunglasses, black gloves, and a majestic white fireman's helmet covered in Mets stickers and buckled with chains beneath his chin. He looks intense, but he's a sweet man.

Lastly, do yourself a favor and try to spot "the Tie Guy," Ernie Searle. He typically wears a bright blue button-down shirt that has a Mets logo on the front pocket. He has the name "Tie Guy" on the back, No. "69" in tape and, of course, he'll be wearing some sort of wild, bright, elaborate Mets tie. "Since I knew there were Mets ties, I started looking for them and finding them and I'd wear a different tie to each game," Searle told WPIX in 2014.

I've also seen him in a Hawaiian-style Mets shirt, orange shorts, bright suspenders, and a variety of white, orange, or blue attire. But the mainstay is the tie. He always has on a Mets tie.

Any section about superfans would be incomplete without mentioning Karl Ehrhardt, "the Sign Man," who died in 2008. He was 83 years old. From 1964 to 1981, Ehrhardt regularly brought a bag of 20-by-26-inch placards to dozens of games at Shea Stadium each year. Depending on what had just happened in the game, Ehrhardt could instantly reach in his bag and pull out a sign that read, "Just Great," or, "Can You Believe It?" or "There Are No Words."

He also had signs for the opposition. He had a "Look Ma, No Hands" sign for when someone would make an error. Or, "Jose, Can You See," for whenever outfielder José Cardenal struck out. TV cameras made a habit of focusing in on him during a game broadcast whenever he unfolded a sign. "I just called them the way I saw them," Ehrhardt told *The New York Times* in 2006.

In total, he said, he made 1,200 signs during his time going to games at Shea Stadium—and he saved all of them. In 2002 the Mets personally invited Mr. Ehrhardt to their 40th anniversary. He sat by the dugout, stood up, and held a sign that read: "The Sign Man Lives."

The diverse dining options at Citi Field include (from left to right) sushi from Daruma of Tokyo, the All-Star Meatball Hero, and "Batter Up" Fried Chicken from Tribeca Grill. (AP Images)

Eat at Citi Field

Bucket Rank: 🗑️ 🗑️ 🗑️ 🗑️

Since its opening, Citi Field has repeatedly ranked as one of the top American stadiums for food. In addition to amazing, exclusive options in left field's Acela Club and Pat LaFrieda's chophouse in the Delta Club, there are tasty options accessible all over and to everyone. "[Citi Field] deserves credit, perhaps more than any other big league park, for making stadium dining a selling point rather than a drawback of the baseball experience," *USA TODAY*'s Ted Berg wrote in early 2016. "Its outfield concourse alone offers a brilliant array of delicious options, from barbecue to burgers to pastrami to sushi to big, beautiful Italian heroes."

David Chang's spicy Fuku sandwich, which costs $12, is worth every penny. The line is almost always short, and the sandwich is consistently perfect. It is crunchy, dense, salty, and spicy and topped with a pickle on a soft, potato bun. Also at Fuku you can get Chang's Milk Bar cookies, the best of which is the Compost Birthday Cake.

Similarly, the Blue Smoke Grilled Barbecue Chicken Sandwich, which can be found in center field, is equally terrific. It's not as crunchy as the Fuku, but that's partly because it is covered in a thin blue cheese dressing that disappears by soaking in to the breading. The mac and cheese and pulled pork are outstanding as well.

Prior to the Fuku chicken, Danny Meyer's El Verano Taqueria was my go-to eatery at Citi Field. The corn tortillas are chewy—in a good way—and they provide just the right amount of structure when smothering the barbacoa or chicken in their spicy cilantro salsa. However, if you can only get one item here, the Mexican corn with spicy mayo, cojita cheese, and cayenne pepper, while messy, is a delight.

It's overly gluttonous, but every Mets fan should experience Pig Guy NYC's Bacon on a Stick. The $8.50, spicy, maple syrup-covered option sounds like it would be terrible, but it's awesome. Every time I have it, I need to announce to everyone in sight just how amazing it is. The S'mores-dipped option is always great, I hear, but too sweet for me.

In less than a minute, you can get one of Mets fan Josh Capon's famous pressed sandwiches, including his sourdough grilled cheese, broccoli rabe with havarti, or bacon and tomato marmalade. If pressed is not your style, I hear people rave about the Italian muffaletta with capicola, mortadella, provolone, and a layer of olive salad. That said, as good as those are, I always defer to the short rib grilled cheese with arugula and tomato jam on a brioche.

Obviously, no list about Citi Field's food would be complete without mentioning Shake Shack. In 2009, when Citi Field opened, its Shake Shack was only the third in existence. Now, Meyer has dozens of locations around the U.S. The Citi Field location also features the Smoke Shack, a unique cheeseburger with Niman Ranch bacon, chopped cherry peppers, and Shack Sauce. But the classic Shack burger is still the best with its crispy, salty exterior and greasy bun. The thing is because Shake Shacks are no longer difficult to find in New York it's hard to justify waiting in the ballpark line. Depending on the crowd size and intensity of the game, the Shake Shack line in center field can run up to two innings' worth of wait time.

Pat LaFrieda's Original Filet Mignon Steak Sandwich is stacked high with 100 percent black angus, hand-cut beef, monterey jack cheese, Vidalia onions, and au jus served on a toasted baguette. There are people I know who believe this is the best food item in the ballpark. Personally, I prefer his meatball sliders with whipped ricotta. Also, his short rib arancini is amazing, but it can only be had in the Delta Sky360 Club.

Two Boots is always a popular choice for pizza. Now located above home plate in the upper level and owned by two passionate Mets fans, Two Boots has a range of uniquely named pies. My favorite will always be the Newman, which includes sopressata and Italian sausage.

The best value in Citi Field is easily the roasted turkey hero with homemade mozzarella and either extra gravy or roasted red peppers and olive oil from Mama's of Corona in right field. It's $12.95, 10 inches long, packed with turkey and cheese, dripping in peppers, fresh, clean, and delicious, and I never finish it in one sitting, which means it can cover for a small snack later in the game as well. It's perfect.

However, while all of the above food is terrific, high quality, and strongly recommended, I always come back to my first love—the Premio Hot Sausage with peppers and onions—especially on a cold night. I try to avoid it, but I'm instinctively reeled in when I get a whiff of those fried peppers and sweet onions. I try to turn back, but the sizzle on the griddle makes it impossible. I also like that when I bite in to this old-school favorite it takes me back to Shea Stadium, where they served it the exact same way.

. . . .

Attend Mets Fantasy Camp

Bucket Rank: 🗑 🗑 🗑

There is roughly a 1 percent chance that a high school baseball player will get drafted by a Major League Baseball team, according to a 2015 study conducted by the Robert Wood Johnson Foundation and the Harvard T.H. Chan School of Public Health. I was among the 99 percent who didn't make it. However, as a right-handed, asthmatic, 5'8" pitcher, that should not have come as a surprise. Nevertheless, I still wonder what it would have been like to put on the uniform and throw to big league hitters.

This is why in the early 1980s, former Chicago Cubs catcher Randy Hundley came up with the idea to create a baseball fantasy camp, where fans—usually 40 and older—can play the game in an authentic uniform alongside former players from their favorite team. Hundley's Cubs were the first team to offer the experience. By 2016 24 of the league's 30 teams offered official fantasy camps for their fans, including the Mets, who host theirs at their spring training complex in Port St. Lucie, Florida.

In exchange for more than $4,500, the package provides transportation from the airport, hotel accommodations in Port

St. Lucie, transportation to and from the field, two personalized, authentic Mets uniforms, breakfast, a buffet lunch, an Opening Night welcome dinner, a mid-week barbecue, an awards dinner, coaching, training, and your own clubhouse locker. The camp's players and participants are also invited back for a reunion game in Citi Field played prior to a Mets game during the regular season. "I go to fantasy camp because it's one of the rare opportunities we get in life to a) relive the past and b) hang out with our childhood heroes without c) really messing up our marriages," said lifelong Mets fan Eric Brown.

Brown is a fantasy camp veteran, having attended multiple since his first in 2005.

"I'm not exaggerating, it was the most fun I've had in my entire life," he told me. "I wasn't alone. All 110 of us were walking around with these ridiculous goofy grins on our faces. It was just so much fun."

In recent years Mets Fantasy Camp has featured middle-aged, former players from multiple eras, including John Stearns, Doug Flynn, Al Jackson, Wally Backman, Dwight Gooden, and Edgardo Alfonzo. And, according to Brown, they all look to be having as much fun playing baseball again as the fans. "They love talking about the game. They love teaching," he explained. "For them I think it's probably— on some small level—a chance to relive their own glory days with people they know will appreciate it."

In spring training of 2014, a former Mets player who had taken part in fantasy camp the previous season confirmed Brown's thinking. "It is incredibly rewarding getting to hear how they remember what we all experienced on field," the player told me, speaking in anonymity. "We lived those great moments, but I only know it from my story. It's great hearing how they saw it and how important it was to their childhood or how my great catch helped a fan forget a problem. That's cool and, especially since for most us—because baseball isn't my everyday life—I think most guys here appreciate hearing those stories as much as the fans like talking about it."

I'm sure it also helps that the former big leaguers are paid $2,500 to $6,000 per week to be there, depending on the popularity of the player. That said, a paycheck and nostalgia are not the only reasons former big leaguers go to fantasy camp.

According to the player I talked with in 2014, who asked to remain anonymous, working fantasy camp is also a great way for guys who drifted out of the game to reconnect with former teammates, as well as network and build relationships that could potentially lead to coaching or scouting positions in the future. In the case of the Mets, their fantasy camp takes place in Port St. Lucie on a field that is 300 yards from where the organization's entire minor league department and in-town front office executives go to work every day.

It's also not just men that go to fantasy camp. Each year, according to the Mets, two to three women will join the 100 men that sign up each session. In 2015 Mets fan and Albany, New York, resident Wendy Shotsky was one of two women in camp. Shotsky, 64, has been a Mets fan since 1962 and told her local newspaper that she wanted to play professional baseball while playing Little League during the late 1950s. "It was also heaven to be able to do it," she said after returning from camp. "I don't kid myself. I'm not very good, but it's fun. When you get a hit, it's a real kick." In January of 2016, the Boston Red Sox held the first ever Women's Fantasy Camp in Fort Myers, Florida, where 48 women were led by former players Trot Nixon, Alan Embree, Brian Daubach, Rich Gedman, and others.

I was invited by the Mets to take part in their 2012 Fantasy Camp as part of a promotional deal through SNY. To prepare I started going to the gym and batting cages multiple times each week during the three months before it was set to begin. Unfortunately, the week before the event, my grandfather passed away, and I also developed pneumonia. I now realize that reads like an unbelievably bad excuse, but I promise it's true and so I never made it down to Florida. I still regret not going. I trained because I didn't want to embarrass myself. In my mind, Gooden, Alfonzo, Backman, and other legends were going to be just as talented and sharp today as they were during their playing

When, Where, and How Much

WHEN: January 15–21 and January 22–28, 2017.

WHERE: Port St. Lucie, Florida.

COST: $4,695.

COST INCLUDES: bus from the airport to the Hilton Garden Inn, seven days/six nights of hotel accommodations, group transportation to and from the hotel each day, two authentic Mets uniforms, daily continental breakfast and buffet lunch, Opening Night welcome dinner, mid-week barbecue, awards dinner with the pros, clubhouse locker, equipment (except gloves and cleats), clubhouse staff and trainers, daily games, personalized baseball cards, fantasy camp video, bull session with the pros, special reunion at Citi Field during a Mets regular season game, and a championship game under the lights at Tradition Field.

days. Obviously, this is impossible; otherwise they'd still be playing, but how can you escape that feeling?

Mets fan and comedian Jim Breuer made the opposite mistake when he booked his trip to go to Mets Fantasy Camp after the 2015 season. "I thought fantasy camp was just meeting ballplayers, taking batting practice, and watching them on the field. I didn't know you played games," he told the *St. Lucie News Tribune* the next spring about his thinking when he first signed up. "So I started training in October. I'm not even exaggerating. I got a personal trainer. It hasn't helped. There's parts on my fingers that I didn't know could ache. There's parts between my back and my heart that I didn't know existed...But hands down, I will be here next year if life allows it."

According to Brown, while some of the former players are in terrific shape and still have impressive talent, there are many instances where fans are actually better than them because of the age difference and current fitness level. Brown said the level and style of play is more relaxed and far less aggressive than rookies fear it will be. For instance, similar to Little League, there is no stealing bases, and players can't advance on pass balls.

The Mets typically offer two separate fantasy camp sessions during the middle of January each winter. By November 14, 2016, their second week of fantasy camp had already been sold out, while the first had limited slots available.

. . . .

Fist Bump Mr. Met

Bucket Rank:

Mr. Met has been the team's official mascot after first being introduced to fans on the cover of game programs, yearbooks, and scorecards in 1963. In 1964, as the Mets moved from the Polo Grounds to Shea Stadium, the team debuted a live costumed version of Mr. Met, who was originally portrayed by team employee and salesperson Daniel J. Reilly. By the mid-1970s, however, with the team struggling to recapture the on-field magic from previous seasons, Mr. Met was less visible.

In 1979 the franchise stopped using Mr. Met altogether and instead experimented with a new mascot, "Mettle the Mule," who was a living animal paraded along the foul lines before a game. Thankfully, this lasted only one season. Finally, in 1994 Mr. Met returned to the Shea Stadium experience but with a head reaching 70 inches in diameter, which is twice the size of what we see on him today.

The Mets also announced that their mascot would now have a new attitude, which was code for copying the antagonistic style of the San Diego Chicken (Padres) and Phillie Phanatic (Phillies), both of whom rose in popularity during the 1980s.

In order to give Mr. Met more personality, his head needed to be large enough to fit levers that the human operator could use to move the mascot's arms, eyebrows, and—if he really wanted to be rude to opposing fans—stick out his tongue.

Mets fan A.J. Mass was hired to play the 1994 version of Mr. Met because he was the only actor able to fit in to the outfit during an audition for a promotional campaign being created by the ballpark. In his first season back, Mr. Met's only on-field responsibility was to dance to "Take Me Out to the Ballgame" alongside nine dancing baseball gloves during the seventh-inning stretch.

The next season, Mets marketing ditched the dancing gloves and asked Mass to spend more time interacting with fans in Shea Stadium. However, Mass told them that it would be nearly impossible to do so given the suit's size and technical limitations. Thanks to Mass, the Mets redesigned the costume, resulting in the mascot we know and love today. To allow Mass to more easily get around the ballpark, designers reduced the size of the mascot's head, eliminated his movable facial features, and went with a permanent smile.

In my view this is a large part of what makes him so enduring to fans because—regardless of what is happening around him, be it rain, heckling, or losing—he is always smiling.

"Mr. Met would do what I did, and that became the character traits," Mass told ESPN during an interview in 2014. "I saw him as childlike, who liked dancing and was there to be friends with the children and root for the Mets, no matter what."

Mass played the team's mascot through 1997, which was his final season beneath the mask. He took advantage of the opportunity. He believes his personality helped set an example for who Mr. Met is and how he behaves today at Citi Field. Mass is right. The early '90s version of Mr. Met was intended to be silly and snarky like other mascots getting attention in ballparks across MLB. However, it was Mass who suggested the new look while working to reshape Mr. Met into an enthusiastic, hopeful character who always believes in the team, which is how most people try to be in the stands.

Mr. Met's rise in national popularity also can be attributed to his brilliant performance in ESPN's series of "This is *SportsCenter*" commercials, which he debuted during 2003. In the first ad, Mr. Met and his wife, Lady Met, are seen driving home after watching a live taping of *SportsCenter*. With "Meet the Mets" playing on the car radio, subtitles read beneath Lady Met: "They should make you a *SportsCenter* anchor. You're much sexier than Scott Van Pelt."

Mr. Met reprised his role in 2009, during which he's seen talking with *SportsCenter* anchor Stuart Scott by a microwave in the break room at ESPN's studios. This is silly in its own right because Mr. Met never speaks, so it's fun to imagine what their conversion must have sounded like. During their conversation, Texas Rangers power-hitting outfielder Josh Hamilton walks in to get lunch, at which point Mr. Met crumples up a Dixie cup, throws it on the ground, angrily gestures at Hamilton, and storms out of the room. Hamilton, fresh off hitting 35 home runs during the Home Run Derby in 2008, asks why Mr. Met is so upset. "A couple of those Home Run Derby balls you hit, they were his cousins," Scott explained.

Mr. Met also appeared in a series of local commercials aired by the Mets in advance of the team returning home from a road trip. The ads all show how Mr. Met kills time at Shea Stadium when the team is out of town. The elevator music in the background is also a nice touch.

My personal favorite has Mr. Met firing T-shirts from his Party Patrol gun at a member of the Shea Stadium ground crew, who is trying to rake dirt on the infield. In an attempt to not be noticed, Mr. Met ducks behind an orange field-level seat. However, since his head is

Mr. Met is popular in part because he seems so enthusiastic and optimistic. (USA TODAY Sports Images)

three feet wide, his noggin and black Mets hat are easily spotted despite his best efforts. "Dude," the team employee, who has a thick New York accent, says. "I can see like 80 percent of your head." The man returns to raking, shaking his head in disapproval, as Mr. Met pops back up to peg him in the back with another T-shirt.

On September 14, 2007, Mr. Met was elected into the Mascot Hall of Fame, where he joined the Coyote of the NBA's San Antonio Spurs, the Gorilla of the NBA's Phoenix Suns, and, of course, his rivals, the Phillie Phanatic and San Diego Chicken. "We just hope it doesn't go to his head," team officials said after the big news.

In 2013 the Mets began wearing batting practice hats with the official 1963 Mr. Met logo on the front. And in 2014 a similar patch was added to their all blue, alternative home and road jersey. In addition to standing on top of dugouts, roaming the stands high-fiving fans, and dancing with Citi Field's Party Patrol between innings, Mr. Met is easiest to find beyond center field. There he frequently spends time with families at Kiddie Field, where fans can meet and pose with him for pictures snapped by a Citi Field photographer. "He does so much charity work. He visits children in local hospitals. He does so much good. Kids and adults love him," team spokesman Jay Horowitz told the *Queens Gazette*.

He can also be rented for special events and private parties. In 2007 a YouTube video of Mr. Met attending a fan's wedding went viral, as it featured him enthusiastically dancing to Punjabi music in a crowd of people who seemed totally unaware of his presence. The video ends with a long shot of the dance floor, which is crowded and dimly lit. The scene looks like any other wedding except for seeing the top half of Mr. Met's baseball head and hat happily bobbing to the beat.

He is currently so popular at Citi Field—not just with kids but with adults—that it's impossible to imagine that he was absent for nearly two decades of the team's existence.

The tunnel that runs beneath the perimeter of Citi Field is a constant curve. It'll lead you by the visiting team's clubhouse doors, the back of the Jackie Robinson Rotunda, the press conference room, the Mets clubhouse, the security offices, and finally to the bullpens. You'll also pass Mr. Met's office.

It's an inconspicuous door. It's off-white, barely noticeable against the cinder block walls just like the rest of the entry points along the outside half of the tunnel. However, next to it in straight white lettering on a small blue sign, it reads: "Mr. Met." This is essentially his clubhouse, where he gets ready for the game.

Head down, hustling to not miss a press conference or moment on field to write about before the game, I typically run this corridor for work. Of course, because of the looping curvature to the hallway, if you're not paying attention, you can easily bump in to someone by accident. One day in May of 2011, I was jogging along the wall and nearly tripped over Mr. Met, who was casually exiting his room. Startled, I began apologizing. Mr. Met waved his gigantic hand to stop me from speaking and then tipped his head sideways as if he were thinking about something specific.

I wasn't sure if I was in trouble because he has a permanent smile and you can never tell if he's happy or sad. He then pointed both of his hands at me, pounded his heart, pretended to type on a keyboard, and gave me two thumbs up. He then walked away but not before giving me a fist bump and patting the top of my head. I believe he was telling me he's a fan of my writing, but unfortunately I'll never know. Better than the truth, though, was having a unique moment with the best mascot of all time. I was 36 years old at the time, but it made me feel like I was six again. That is the power of Mr. Met.

Grow a Mustache Like Keith Hernandez

Bucket Rank: 🗑 🗑

Keith Hernandez's legacy is more than just his mustache. In over 8,500 plate appearances, he was a career .296 hitter, including .297 with the Mets. He was a batting champion, world champion, 11-time Gold Glove winner, co-MVP, five-time All-Star, and the best first baseman the Mets ever had. But let's be honest, when it comes to the legend of Hernandez, the mustache has a lot to do with it. "His mustache is an entity and a signature," said *The New York Times'* media writer Richard Sandomir. "It is the thicker, longer cousin to his eyebrows, the hirsute geometric center of his face."

He has said he began growing the mustache when he was 18, though he would shave it off every three years because "it wasn't very mature." In 1977 he was forced to shave it due to a no-facial-hair policy by the St. Louis Cardinals, with whom he broke in to the league three years earlier. He grew it back for a *Sports Illustrated* cover shoot two years later when he was named co-MVP in the National League during 1979.

He only went mustache-less once during his time playing for the Mets, who acquired Hernandez from the Cardinals in 1983. In the midst of an 8-for-41 slump, he shaved on June 10, 1987, in hopes of changing things up. He belted two home runs the next game and hit .389 the rest of the week.

In 2007 Hernandez was left off the American Mustache Institute (AMI)'s Top Sports Mustache of All Time tournament. However, there was an option for write-in candidates. Naturally, I took to

MetsBlog.com and encouraged my fans to flood the site with his name. Sure enough, he was added to the bracket and advanced to the finals, where he defeated Rollie Fingers by 8 percentage points. "While our certified mustacheologists share concerns that the voting may have been more about the man rather than the mustache in Keith's case—fans of sport and mustaches have spoken," AMI executive director Aaron Perlut said in a press release after the context. "The candidacy for Hernandez was also buoyed by an appeal to voters by New York-area media including MetsBlog.com."

Nice! You're welcome, Keith. I'm sure this was the highlight of your professional career.

In 1992, two years after he retired, Hernandez did a two-episode arc on *Seinfeld*. In the episodes titled "The Boyfriend: Part 1" and "The Boyfriend: Part 2," he plays himself and the love interest of Elaine Benes. During the episodes he uttered the memorable phrase, "I'm Keith Hernandez," which he says to himself while searching for the courage to kiss Benes, who was played by Julia Louis-Dreyfus. In 2006 Rob Perri directed a tongue-in-cheek, semi-serious, but oddly poignant short film titled *I'm Keith Hernandez*, which was screened at more than 20 film festivals after its release. According to Perri's website, he chose Hernandez to be the subject of his movie because his mustache is the perfect symbol of "male virility."

Hernandez also appeared in the series finale of *Seinfeld*. According to a 2015 story in *The* (Bergen County, New Jersey) *Record*, he still makes roughly $3,000 a year from the show's syndication rights. He has said on record multiple times that he never had interest in acting. However, in addition to *Seinfeld*, he appeared in one episode of *Law & Order* during 1994, as well as four episodes of *Ghostwriter* in 1993. He also played himself in two movies, *The Scout* (1994) and *The Yards* (2000).

Hernandez was joined by MSG broadcaster Walt "Clyde" Frazier in a series of TV commercials endorsing Just for Men's Mustache and Beard Brush-In Color Gel. In the first ad, the duo act as on-air sports color commentators breaking down the pick-up moves of a man they call, "Mr. Graybeard." In a 2008 follow-up, former Cowboys running back Emmitt Smith became the target of their analysis. "Your beard is weird," Hernandez said, referring to the gray in Smith's beard.

According to *The New York Times*, Hernandez's contract with Just for Men required him to keep his legendary mustache its original jet black. And to ensure its spokesman remained true to the product, they had two executives monitoring Mets games to be sure Hernandez did not let himself turn in to Mr. Gray.

In 2012 Just for Men's parent company, Combe Inc., dropped Hernandez and Frasier from their ad campaign in favor of a different strategy. As a result Hernandez stopped dying his mustache, and for

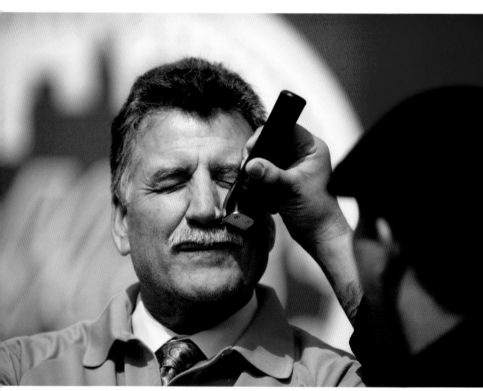

Keith Hernandez raised thousands of dollars for charity in 2012 by having his glorious and famous mustache shaved off. (AP Images)

the first time since growing it when he was 18 years old, it started turning gray. Hernandez started complaining on air during Mets games that he didn't like the way it looked, suggesting he might even go so far as to shave the iconic mustache from his face.

"I'm not totally happy with the gray," he said. "It's something I have to get used to. However, some people on the female side tell me they prefer it gray."

Later that season, 25 years after first growing it, Hernandez shaved the mustache off for charity at a Schick-sponsored event outside of Citi Field. SNY's website, SNY.TV, aired the event live online. Schick donated $5,000 to Hernandez's adult day care facility, and fans were later able to enter a contest to win the razor he used to shave.

In less than two years, Hernandez came to his senses, signed a new deal with Just for Men, grew his mustache back, dyed it black, and restored order to the Mets universe.

. . . .

Experience the 7 Line

Bucket Rank: 🗑 🗑 🗑 🗑

For people who do not do it every day, the ride in to Citi Field on the 7 line train is easy, often illuminating, and a great way to get excited for the game you're about to attend. The station for Citi Field—Mets Stadium-Willet's Point—is located two flights of stairs and roughly 200 feet from the Home Run Apple on Mets Plaza outside of the ballpark. The only way it could be more convenient is if the train literally stopped at your seat.

The 7 train is also the inspiration for The 7 Line Army, a massive contingent of Mets fans brought together through group outings arranged by "The 7 Line," a local T-shirt business run by Darren Meenan. A Mets fan his entire life, Meenan started the company around 2009 after getting traction with his BMX clothing line, Manmade. It was a long and winding road for Meenan, but today The 7 Line has a kiosk in Citi Field and nearly 100 items available for purchase at his website, the7line.com.

Meenan is a brilliant small business owner and marketer, but his greatest talent may be the way he brings Mets fans together before and during games. In 2012, for the last game of the year, Meenan bundled tickets and a T-shirt together in one purchase. It was a huge success and caught the eye of the team when he single-handedly filled the entire Big Apple Reserve with about 600 loud, passionate Mets fans.

In the three seasons since, he has arranged another 45 group outings at Citi Field, and each was attended by 859 fans. They have also gone to 17 outings in road ballparks, including trips to San Francisco, Yankee Stadium, San Diego, Colorado, and Milwaukee. His tentative schedule for 2017 features a similar number of home games, including planned road trips to Washington, D.C., St. Louis, Seattle, and Houston.

To kill time before their group outings, The 7 Line Army sets up a sprawling tailgate in the MTA parking lot below the Mets Stadium/Willet's Point train platform. I've been to several, including during all the 2015 postseason games, and it's a lot of fun. The people are great, especially to newcomers. I'm happy to say I've met several people there who eventually became close friends, including Meenan. His group is easy to spot if you want to meet up. Just look for a hundred or so Mets fans all happy to be wearing orange. They eat, drink, and play games below a giant flag 30 feet in the air that reads, "The 7 Line Army."

If you board the train in Manhattan, it will exit the subway tunnel in Long Island City, quickly passing the Queensboro Bridge and Silvercup Studios, which is where *The Sopranos*, *Mad Men*, and *Sex and the City* were filmed. The ride rumbles along, zigzagging through local neighborhoods, including Astoria, Jackson Heights, Corona, and eventually Flushing. According to the last U.S. census, the population of Queens is almost 50 percent immigrant. That means if Queens was a city, it would have the highest percentage of immigrants in the country, and the train ride offers a terrific example of New York and America, showcasing a beautiful melting pot of different cultures and experiences, traveling in the same direction. "Astoria is home to many Greeks and Egyptians, Woodside has one of the largest populations of Irish immigrants in the country, Corona is home to many Mexican and other Latin American immigrants, and Flushing's Chinatown is much larger than what remains in Manhattan, and is decidedly less China about its town-ness with Korean, Vietnamese, and other recent Asian immigrants," John Giuffo wrote for Forbes. com in a 2012 article about traveling to the MLB All-Star Game.

In late 1999 Atlanta Braves closer John Rocker made a series of racist and offensive comments to *Sports Illustrated* about the diverse community that peacefully rides the train together every day to Shea Stadium. He was rightfully ridiculed for his remarks by national media and threatened by fans at Shea. Thankfully, countless fans and players continue to take the train to Citi Field every game despite Rocker's ignorant, personal opinions.

In 2006 I took the train to Shea on a busy Friday afternoon. It was crowded, so I stood, holding a bar for support. It was a bouncy, 40-minute ride from Grand Central Terminal. As I stood waiting for the last set of doors to open, I noticed Mets reliever Heath Bell standing to my right. He had apparently been sitting next to me the entire ride. It is not uncommon to see players commuting. Each season, just like their fellow New York residents, there are several Mets players who choose to take the subway to work.

For the most part, the players riding the train are young and not yet earning a big enough salary to afford paying to park a car in the city, which can cost as much as $500 a month depending on the neighborhood. If that's the case, he'll often choose to leave the car at his offseason home and ride the 7 train instead.

That being said, it's not just less-than-famous younger guys who ride the rails. I've heard fans and media over the years mention seeing all sorts of high-profile players getting off the 7 train, including Ron Darling, Al Leiter, John Olerud, David Wright, Carlos Delgado, and Daniel Murphy. "I took it every year during the '80s," Darling told me. "Eventually, I got a car, which I thought was great until I realized how much it would cost for parking."

The ride leaving Citi Field to Manhattan provides a breathtaking view of the New York skyline, especially when coming back from a day game around sunset. The ride from Manhattan to Citi Field will cost you just $2.75 on the 7 train and it will keep you moving. Plus, as Darling said, it's a lot better than paying for parking.

Mets players usually arrive to the ballpark for a night game around 2:00 to 2:30 PM, so the train getting them to Citi Field is fairly empty. Unfortunately, leaving the stadium can be a different story. If it's a nail-biting, important nine-inning game that is riveting until the final out, meaning no fans left early and will all be leaving Citi Field at the same time, the train platform can get crowded and crazy.

In the 2016 postseason, thousands of fans were left to funnel themselves up and down a 40-foot stairwell and through 10 turnstiles, after which waves of trains picked up bunches of fans while leaving others behind to get the next one...and the next one... and the next one. It took hours to empty out.

It, though, used to be significantly worse at Shea Stadium. The new platform for Citi Field is more spacious and less winding, so it flows better than before. However, on those extra busy nights, it is still a madhouse. But, if the Mets win, even the craziest subway scramble can be entertaining, as pumped-up fans lead chants, high-five each other, and crack jokes.

The players wisely wait this out. A veteran player on the Mets recently told me his teammates who take the train are always the last to leave since they usually wait until the last fan exits the ballpark before they consider heading out for their ride home.

. . . .

Learn a Lesson from Bill Buckner

Bucket Rank: 🗑 🗑

Boston Red Sox first baseman Bill Buckner's baseball career will forever be remembered for one play, especially among Mets fans. In Game 6 of the 1986 World Series, Buckner, who had been hampered by knee problems all season, was unable to stop a slow, bouncing ground ball from Mookie Wilson. The ball went between Buckner's legs and allowed the winning run to score from third base.

In September of 2016, I met Buckner after he filmed a promo spot with Wilson for the MLB Network. In the quick, 30-second commercial, Buckner (dressed in a red shirt) and Wilson (dressed in a blue shirt) spend the day together, during which Bill makes a series of routine, everyday catches, such as snagging an apple from a street vendor, a falling plant from an old lady's window, and a flying frisbee in the park. The bit ends with Wilson and Buckner walking across a Little League field. A batted ball rolls toward them and stops just before reaching their feet. The two men look at it, then look at one another, and laugh like old friends.

It took time, but Buckner now has a sense of humor and an insightful perspective about the moment that altered his legacy and helped the Mets win their second World Series. He smiled when we talked that day at MLB Network. He was humble, affable, and honest. He appeared reasonable and measured.

So, I went for it…

"Well, look, I have to say it," I said. "Thank you. Thank you for making the error."

He laughed but did it sort of embarrassingly. Also, he clearly had heard it all before. But I continued. "I'm sure it wasn't easy for you, going through everything that transpired. But for me, as a 10 year old, it wasn't just a baseball game. It was a lesson in life about persistence and never giving up. It had a profound impact on me. My parents were always fighting when I was a kid. I felt alone as an only child and didn't have a lot of hope inside. But seeing that moment, watching the Mets win the way they did when everything seemed hopeless, at 10 years old, you guys taught me that anything is possible, to never give up, and when things seem dark, it could be because there is light around the corner. So while I have no doubt that you dealt with a lot of pain because of it, and it probably changed your life to a certain extent, know that for me it also changed my life. And for that I'm thankful."

He shook my hand, smiled, and slightly nodded his head. "I promise there are a lot worse things in life than making an error and losing a baseball game," he said. "It wasn't fun, but it taught me to try and see everything in a positive way because, like you're saying, it's there if you try to find it."

Buckner was drafted out of high school by the Los Angeles Dodgers, with whom he got to the big leagues a year later. He was later traded to the Chicago Cubs in a five-player deal in 1977. In his fourth season in Chicago, Buckner hit .324 and won the National League batting title. He made his only appearance in an All-Star Game the next season. In 1984 he had become a bench player for the Cubs, and Buckner was traded to the Red Sox and immediately became their starting first baseman. In 1985 he played in 162 games at first base while driving in 110 runs.

Then came 1986, when Buckner hit .267 with 18 home runs, 39 doubles, and 102 RBIs to help the Red Sox to get to the playoffs for the first time in 11 years. It was his 18th season in the big leagues. "The dreams are that you're gonna have a great series and win. The nightmares are that you're gonna let the winning run score on a ground ball through your legs," Buckner told WBZ-TV 19 days before Game 6, according to Dan Shaughnessy's 1997 book *At Fenway: Dispatches from Red Sox Nation.*

The Red Sox held a 3–2 series lead over the Mets, entering Game 6 of the World Series, and were one win away from their first championship in 68 years. In the seventh inning, Red Sox starter pitcher Roger Clemens was removed from the game with a blister on his finger. He was cruising, having allowed just two runs. His replacement, Calvin Schiraldi, instantly gave up a run in the eighth inning that allowed the Mets to tie the game. Eleven months earlier the Mets traded Schiraldi to the Red Sox for Bob Ojeda, who allowed just three runs in 13 innings against Boston during the series.

The Red Sox went up 5–3 in the top of the 10th inning, putting them three outs away from a series win. However, Schiraldi, who was still in the game, surrendered singles to Gary Carter, Kevin Mitchell, and Ray Knight. Carter scored, after which Schiraldi was replaced with Bob Stanley. With two strikes and two outs, champagne on ice, and Sox players and fans braced for a win, Stanley threw a wild pitch, allowing the tying run to score. Wilson then hit a slow roller down the first-base line that went underneath Buckner's glove, through his legs, and into right field. Knight scored from the third, Boston lost, and the Mets won.

Buckner stood tall with his hands behind his head and watched in disbelief as the Mets celebrated at home plate. "I thought, *What is going on,*" Buckner told reporters at Shea Stadium in 2006, when

Bill Buckner poses with Mookie Wilson, who hit the ball that went between Buckner's legs during Game 6 of the 1986 World Series. (AP Images)

asked about the moment. "I turned around to go after the ball and realized the game was over."

Two days later the Mets went on to win Game 7 and the World Series. Buckner was released by the Red Sox and signed by the California Angels midway through the next season. After that infamous Game 6 play, life in Boston had gotten rough for Buckner. "People were pretty mean, pretty rude, even to my family, which really bothered me," Buckner told me.

In time, partly because of the abuse, he left Massachusetts to live full time in Idaho, where he had owned a ranch since 1975. Today he owns several businesses and some real estate and earns a supplemental income with Wilson from signing pictures and memorabilia about his infamous Game 6 moment. "It took a long time for me to decide whether I wanted to do it or not," Buckner told ESPN.com in 2006. "And the more I thought about it, I thought, *Well, you know what, I have taken a lot of heat over this, so I might as well get something out of it.* I thought it would be a one or two-time thing. I had no idea that I could put all my kids through college just by signing the pictures."

In hindsight, I should also send thank you notes to Clemens for developing a game-changing blister. I should thank then-Mets general manager Frank Cashen for sending Schiraldi to the Red Sox. And thank Schiraldi for letting the game be tied, so Stanley could throw a wild pitch. I guess I should thank Stanley, too.

The point is there were a lot of moments and men who contributed to the outcome of that game. It wasn't just Buckner. However, fair or unfair, he is who we all identify with for that game. He carries the weight and he has carried it well and with pride. He's a strong man to be able to take that kind of abuse, smile, and turn it in to a positive.

Name Your Kid Shea

Bucket Rank: 🗑️ 🗑️

In July of 2016, Mets third baseman David Wright and his wife, Molly, welcomed their first child into the world. Fittingly, her middle name is Shea. "It was actually my wife's idea," Wright told me. "She knew it was important for me to honor the relationship I have with the organization and fanbase that has given us so much. Plus she loved the name Shea, so it wasn't difficult to convince her."

In 1969, according to the Social Security Administration, there was a spike in Connecticut, New York, and New Jersey among people naming their newborn child Shea. A similar spike occurred in the same region just after 1986. The reason is obvious, as these are the two years the Mets popped champagne after winning their only two world championships. According to *The Wall Street Journal*'s Andrew Beaton, "Whenever they're excited about the team, the popularity of the name Shea surges."

Surprisingly, more babies were named Shea during the 2000s than any other decade, which is odd considering the Mets hadn't won a World Series in more than 15 years. However, they did get to the postseason in 1999 and lost in the World Series to the New York Yankees in 2000. Also, they got to the National League Championship Series in 2006 and played their last game in Shea Stadium at the end of 2008.

Interestingly, among the people during the 2000s to name their child Shea, was legendary Atlanta Braves third baseman Chipper Jones, who was reviled by Mets fans. In 2004 Jones told New York reporters that he didn't name his newborn son Shea because of the stadium; instead he simply loved the name. "My wife did, too," he insisted, talking to media in the Shea Stadium dugout. "A lot of people think

I was doing it just to get at the Mets fans, but that's not the case…I could've played in the American League my whole career and I still would have named him Shea."

For what it's worth, in 88 games at Shea Stadium during his career, Jones hit .313 with 19 home runs. That's more than he hit in any road ballpark. "I love playing there," Jones once said of Shea Stadium. "Check the numbers."

No kidding, Chipper. To be honest, my biggest fear is that Chipper's son, Shea, will grow up resentful of the Mets, become a big league player, suit up for the Braves, and do more damage in Citi Field than even his dad did in Shea. Of course, after hitting 100 home runs in Citi Field, Shea Jones will eventually name his son, Citi, and continue the cycle.

Cincinnati Reds shortstop Barry Larkin also included Shea in his daughter's middle name but was brave enough to admit it was an homage to the Mets, for whom he never played but did torment in their ballpark. "I loved Shea Stadium," he told AOL.com in 2015. "I wanted to be a fighter pilot when I was a kid, so the roar of the engines [over Shea Stadium] always did something for me. Whenever the planes would fly over my head, it would energize me. I'm sitting there at short or I'm hitting and I can feel the roar of the engine. That and the fans—I loved playing there, just loved it."

Larkin hit .285 with 19 extra base hits and 28 RBIs in 66 games at Shea during his 19-year career. In 2014 actor, comedian, and overt Mets fan Kevin James and his wife, Steffiana, gave birth to their second child, Shea Joelle, on June 14. "I have been a Mets fan my whole life and have such good memories going to Shea Stadium," he told *People* magazine when asked about his daughter's name. "I can't believe this got by my wife. She ended up liking the name just for the name itself."

Interestingly, among the more than 1,800 people named Shea during the last hundred years, 54 percent are female, and 46 percent are male. Going along with those percentages was Mets fan Andrew

Guckian, who gave his daughter, Bailey, the middle name of Shea in 2009. His wife was a proponent for the name as well. "We were both on the same page with it, from the get go," he told me. "Bailey is six now and knows the reason we used the name. Thankfully, my girls love going to games as much as we do, so while it's not something she seems to care about, there is an attachment there."

In honor of his father, who died in 2012, Mets fan Jeremiah LeClerc also used Shea as his daughter's middle name. "My father, Roger, was a lifelong Mets fan and he passed down that wonderful gift to me," Jeremiah explained. "My wife is actually a Pirates fan, but she's very understanding about my severe love of the Mets. She was actually the one who brought up the name Shea for our daughter's middle name. She knew what a wonderful man my father was and how much he affected my life and thought it would be a nice and clever way to honor him."

The 2010s are getting off to a good start as well with 98 babies being named Shea in 2011. And with the Mets getting to the World Series in 2015, perhaps more will follow.

Run the Mr. Met Dash

Bucket Rank: 🗑️ 🗑️

Every Sunday following afternoon games, the Mets run the Mr. Met Dash, during which children ages 12 and under can run the bases at Citi Field. In advance of the event, guests looking to participate are asked to exit the ballpark and form a line outside the Bullpen Gate on 126th Street immediately after the game concludes.

According to fans that haven taken part, it's smart to leave the game and get in line as early as the seventh inning, though some fans clearly head down even earlier than that. Depending on that day's attendance, the line can back up through the parking lot to the steps leading up to the Mets Stadium/Willets Point train station. So in total, if you and your kids are last in line at the time they start the event, it could take up to an hour to get inside the stadium and finish running the bases. This whole process may sound tedious and overwhelming, but every fan I know who has done this loves it. The kids all love it. And the parents love it, especially since Mom and Dad get to go on the field, too, where they stand just off the grass as their child sprints in a 360-foot circle with a smile.

It's worth noting that members of Mr. Met's Kids Club get to jump the line. The Kids Club is a special program for children under 14. It has two membership levels. Blue memberships are free and come with four free Sunday ticket vouchers. All-Star memberships cost $33. In 2017 an MVP membership costs $53 and you four free Sunday ticket vouchers for the field level. Both memberships include a T-shirt, stickers, prizes, a scoreboard message, and, of course, a front-of-the-line pass for unlimited Mr. Met Dashes.

In general Sunday is more or less family day at Citi Field. If you're taking your kid to a game, Sunday is the day to go. In addition to the dash, they have bounce houses, face painters, and balloon artists on the Mets Plaza before each game, plus giveaways for the first 15,000 fans.

According to Matthew Silverman's book, *Best Mets*, the Mr. Met Dash started in the mid-1990s at Shea Stadium, where it was previously called the "Dyna-Mets Dash," as well as the "Kids Dash."

My friend, Maggie Wiggin, ran the dash at Shea when she was 10 years old. "It was a lot of fun; it felt important," she said. Wiggin continued the tradition by letting her two-year-old son, Tommy, run the Mr. Met Dash at Citi Field in 2016. "It was amazing to see him make the connection between what he had watched [from the stands] and what he was doing," she said of the experience. "He was almost overwhelmed just looking around the huge stadium, but he also seemed to understand his 'job' and ran the base paths without much guidance."

It's different each time, but at some point along the way, kids rounding first, second, or third base get to high-five Mr. Met. "He got completely star struck when he passed Mr. Met and stopped and stared at him slack-jawed. He's a real celebrity in our house," Wiggin said earnestly.

Mom and Dad can snap a quick picture of the special moment. However, be ready. Don't fumble your camera because things move fast and stop for no one. Mets fan Bryan Curry takes his son, Sean (10), and daughter, Mackenzie (eight), to the dash two to three times a season. "My son is in awe as soon as he steps on the field. It's his dream to get to play there one day," Curry told me. "I have to keep reminding him that he can't slide into home or he might hurt someone and they won't let him run the bases anymore."

In the decade I've had press credentials, I always continue to pinch myself when I walk through the dugout, up the steps, and on to the field. There is no pitch; everything is at eye level. There is no distance; everything is up close. It's a colorful experience—vivid and larger than life. The other media members, and especially the players and coaches, slowly strut like it's no big deal. They're probably used to it. I should be used to it, too, by now, but I'm not. I'm still an unabashed Mets fan, who just happens to be media.

When I was a kid, I would have done anything imaginable to be able to sit quietly in the dugout at Shea Stadium with the sun setting in the distance, watching these people go to work. Now I can, and that will never be lost on me. But unlike most people, I'm very fortunate to be able to write a blog and get press credentials through SNY. So if given the opportunity to step on the field, on the dirt, under the sun, even at the expense of waiting in line for an hour so your kid can run the bases, you should do it. It'll be fun for your child. But let's be honest, it'll be really fun for you, too. "You get an appreciation for how grand and intimate the stadium actually is," Nate Kiel, 36, from Manhattan told me about his experience running the dash with his child. "The distance between the bases, the size of the stands and scoreboard, and how the seats appear to encroach all around you, it's something I'll never forget."

When the Mr. Met Dash is over, ushers escort you and your family out of the building by going through the tunnel that runs under and around Citi Field. The parents I know that have done this all marvel at being inside, under the stadium and seeing where players, media, and team executives routinely begin and end their day.

• •

Tour Citi Field

Bucket Rank: 🗑 🗑 🗑 🗑

In 2010 the Mets started offering fans a guided walking tour of Citi Field during weekend afternoons when the team is playing on the road. The tour gives fans a behind-the-scenes look at the press box, production areas, bullpen, and the ballpark's finest suites. However, the highlight of the trip is getting to step on field, walk the warning track, go in the Mets clubhouse, and take photos in their dugout. In 2016 adults tickets cost $13 with discounts available for children, seniors, and men and women of the military. The tour is free for season-ticket holders. "We've had great interest from our fans since opening the ballpark and we are delighted to be able to provide them a closer look at their team's home," said Mets executive of business operation Dave Howard when the program was first announced.

The tour takes roughly 60 minutes or so to complete. And every person I know that has done it says it's the best $13 a fan can spend in the ballpark. "It was well worth the time and investment," Michael Parker, 41, told me in 2016 outside Citi Field immediately after finishing the tour with his wife and two children. "The Mets take their lumps in the media, but this was so well done. They don't get nearly enough credit for how awesome of an experience this is."

The tour group first meets in the Jackie Robinson Rotunda. There is a stark contrast between seeing two dozen fans waiting patiently—compared to the hour before a game, when hundreds and hundreds of antsy people flood the room on their way up escalators to their seats. It's so quiet and peaceful that there is an echo against the marble walls before the tour, allowing ample time to step back and notice the incredible work and details put in to building enormous, inspiring tributes to Brooklyn legend Jackie Robinson.

After the rotunda the tour takes an elevator up to the press box. This is most fun for fans who are aware of their local reporters, especially people who interact with them on Twitter. It's here where their words get written, which is fun to consider when walking through what is otherwise just a really nice view of the field with rows of empty chairs, outlets, and desk space.

The press box's hidden gem, though, is on its inside wall, which is lined with framed, black-and-white headshots of people the Mets consider their collection of Hall of Fame reporters during the last 50 years. The images are all from each journalist's rookie year on the beat, using the original photo submitted when first getting press credentials. It is a wonderful, often-hilarious collection of bad hair, uncomfortable expressions, and unique clothing. I laugh about it, but it's all in good fun and a sweet tribute to the men and women who do an outstanding job communicating with us every day via print, radio, or TV.

Next up is Citi Field's scoreboard control room, where in-game video entertainment, scoreboard, and music is coordinated with public address announcements, at-bats, and meaningful moments during the game. Similar to the press box, the room has an amazing view of the field but is jam packed with blinking lights, monitors, wires, buttons, and mixing boards. I like to think of it as Citi Field's brain stem. This is also where you'll find the button that launches the Home Run Apple after a home run.

The moment a ball is officially scored a home run, the operator sticks a key into a slot. The key is turned toward the right, which flips open a hatch that contains a button. When that button is pressed, it raises the apple. "It's one step below the nuclear codes," Joe DeVito, the team's executive producer of entertainment, marketing, and production said in an ABC News report.

The guide then exits the brain stem and leads the tour group through a variety of exclusive suites, boxes, and clubs, after which they end up at the seats directly behind home plate. It's now time to step on the field. The tour guide opens the black gate, which is built in to the backstop just off the rolling billboard that fans see behind a batter during the game. The dirt is darker than it looks on TV and it's packed down like pavement. Obviously, this is an incredible opportunity for photographs since fans can finally take a picture with a ground floor, eye-level view of the field they ordinarily gaze at from above.

There is only a short walk along the backstop before being able to take five steps down in to the dugout. The first thing that catches every eye is the row of helmets and bats used by the players during games. However, the other celebrity object in the dugout is the bullpen and review phones, which still have cords and are wired to the wall.

In the dugout the tour guide is certain to show off the bench and the air conditioning and heaters below it. Attention is always paid to the buckets of bubble gum, sunflower seeds, and Gatorade jugs, as well as the video monitors where the manager can see what is happening in the bullpen. It's amazing to be there. This is where we all wanted to be as kids when fantasizing about being big league players in our backyards. With my job I may not be getting an at-bat, but I'm a lot closer than most fans will ever get to the action and I never take that privilege for granted. I see this same look in people's eyes when on the tour. It's clear that each guest walking on the dugout's speckled ground understands just how magical and unique a moment they are experiencing.

The tour then goes up the steps at the opposite end of the dugout, on to the field, and along the warning track to the team's bullpens. Be careful here because people tend to clumsily bump in to each other; after all, it's impossible not to look up and around while walking along the outfield wall. The view from this angle is jaw-dropping. It is an unobstructed perspective that most fans never get to see. It's also worth dragging fingers along the outfield wall, just to know how it might feel to rob a home run.

Similar to the dugout, most everyone on the tour is eager to see the bullpen phone. It is located inside a secure, black box on the wall just as it is in the dugout. The box has large white stickers on the outside that spell "TELEPHONE," I guess in case a coach ever gets confused.

At this point fans on the tour are asked to stop taking pictures because they'll be walking inside and under the stadium before hitting their final stop.

If you take the tour, while walking the long hallway, be sure to look up. There is a mind-boggling number of wires, chords, and cables running above the entire 10,000-foot corridor. It's geeky but rather impressive when you consider all that has to happen to power Citi Field. It's a quick walk before the tour guide stops, turns right, and opens the door to the team's weight room. It looks like any other gym complete with machines, weights, and mirrors, but it also has gigantic blue and orange Mets logos on the wall.

Next up is the team's dining area, where they eat breakfast, lunch, and dinner prepared by Theresa Corderi and her staff. Her food is outstanding, by the way. I eat it every day during spring training, where she also prepares lunch for media covering the team. Her father, who helps her only during spring training, makes the best grilled vegetables, chicken, and steak that I've ever eaten. And when players go hunting or fishing before the season, he'll cook up whatever they bring in as well.

Corderi and her family have been preparing meals for the Mets since 2000. It's an important, never-ending job since she's feeding young professional athletes charged with taking the ultimate care of their bodies. Finally, about an hour in to the tour and after walking through the players' lounge, fans are led into the team's clubhouse. There is so much to take in from the larger-than-expected sets of lockers—what's inside them and where they're located—to the Herman Miller office chairs, dark leather sofas, off-white end tables, and tall ceilings.

The most unique element in the clubhouse is the carpet, which is vibrant, busy, black, and covered with giant baseballs. In between each ball are the neon stick figure drawings that used to line the outside of Shea Stadium. I'm pretty sure every die-hard fan that has walked through the room has wondered how this flooring might look in their home. Unfortunately, it's not for sale...

If time permits, the guide will lead the group through the team's press conference room, which is where pregame and postgame interviews are broadcast on SNY. The tour always ends by again walking back through an empty Jackie Robinson Rotunda to the team's Hall of Fame Museum and clubhouse shop. Here, fans can check out memorabilia, buy merchandise, and say good-bye before

When, Where, and How Much

WHEN: Dates and times change regularly.

WHERE: Depart from Jackie Robinson Rotunda.

COST: $13 for adults, $9 for children (12 and under), $9 for seniors (60 and over). Season-ticket holders and active military get complimentary tickets.

exiting into the parking lot where they can head home or wait an hour or so before re-entering for that night's game.

For just $13, any fan, I'm sure, would want to experience all of the above. It is more than worth your time and something everyone should do at least once.

. . . .

Throw Out the First Pitch

Bucket Rank: 🗑 🗑 🗑 🗑 🗑

In most instances celebrities, politicians, famous athletes, and friends of sponsors get to throw out the ceremonial first pitch to a Major League Baseball game. However, the Mets do a terrific job showcasing local heroes and servicemen and women, as well as regular fans, inviting them to stand center stage, meet players, and be acknowledged as an important part of New York City's and the team's community.

In the last year, NYPD officers, members of FDNY, and families affected by 9/11 have all thrown out the first pitch before a Mets game at Citi Field. In what is a wonderful moment, Mets fans in attendance always cheer them on with a standing ovation while showing appreciation.

In most cases the first-pitch thrower reaches the catcher, who will squat behind home plate ready for anything. The ball may bounce, it may dribble, but it usually gets to the catcher.

However, in the case of rapper 50 Cent and Gary Dell'Abate, Howard Stern's longtime producer, it didn't work out so well. The duo have the distinct honor of having thrown the worst first pitches in Mets history.

In 2014 Curtis "50 Cent" Jackson, who was born in Queens but claims to be a New York Yankees fan, was invited to throw out a first pitch to promote his upcoming summer concert at Citi Field. Jackson used a 1930s, Bob Feller-like delivery, but the lefty-throwing rapper released his pitch wide, sailing the ball at team photographers standing on the first-base line, all of whom were documenting the moment. Jackson was mocked all across the entertainment world. He brushed it off well, later admitting he doesn't care very much about baseball, and that it was simply a fleeting moment between record album sales.

For Dell'Abate it has been far more difficult to live down because he works on Stern's influential SiriusXM satellite radio show, which is heard all over the world. Unlike 50 Cent, Dell'Abate is a loud and proud, die-hard Mets fan. He frequently talked on air about preparing himself for his once-in-a-lifetime moment on the mound at Citi Field. He finally stepped on field during May of 2009. He reared back, smiled, and let his ball fly several feet over and to the left of the catcher before it ultimately landed, hitting the umpire in the leg.

Stern's staff had already been filling ample air time for three decades goofing on Dell'Abate. His first pitch blunder only added fuel to their fire. Dell'Abate's pitch was so bad that—on the moment's 10-year anniversary—Stern's producers created a four-minute, ESPN-style *30 for 30* parody featuring appearances by Jimmy Kimmel, Peter Gammons, and Dan Patrick, among other famous reporters and sports personalities. In the last year, more than 2,400 fans have signed an online petition asking the Mets to give Dell'Abate a chance to redeem himself, but so far the team has not issued an invite to the Stern producer.

Other celebrities have done amazingly well, especially during 2016, including New Jersey native and Olympic gold medalist Laurie Hernandez, who threw out the first pitch during a game in early September of 2016. In true Olympic gymnastics fashion, the 16-year-old Hernandez cartwheeled across the mound before throwing a strike to home plate, earning a standing ovation from the Citi Field crowd.

Also in 2016 tennis legend John McEnroe, who is a Queens native and passionate Mets fan, was invited to throw the ceremonial first pitch before a Mets-Yankees game on ESPN in early August. With gray hair and an all-blue Mets jersey, McEnroe, 57, laser-beamed a perfect strike on the outside corner of home plate, which left broadcasters and fans in stunned disbelief.

However, the best first pitch at Citi Field in 2016 came from five-year-old Ashtin Gerberg, who became known as "Mini Thor" after the Mets tweeted a video of him—looking exactly like Noah Syndergaard—playing catch with his dad a few weeks earlier. In his oversized Mets jersey and long blonde hair, Gerberg amazingly one-hopped his pitch 60 feet to home plate. He later got to meet his idol, Syndergaard, who played catch with him in the outfield before the game.

The opportunity to throw out the ceremonial first pitch is also offered to average fans, as long as they organize a group outing to Citi Field with more than 500 people attending. Mets fan Keith Blacknick used a similar ticketing opportunity to throw out the first pitch before a game during the summer of 2016. Blacknick told me he only prepared for his pitch the day before he was set to throw. He practiced for an hour in the parking lot where he worked, but that was it. The next time he picked up a baseball was his big moment in Citi Field. "I did not stand on the pitching rubber when I threw it because I didn't want to cause any bad luck or be disrespectful to players who can actually play the game," he said of the moment he stepped on the mound. "It was surreal. All I kept thinking to myself was don't be like Dell'Abate or 50 Cent."

Wearing shorts and a 1986 home Mets jersey sporting No. 25, Blacknick's pitch was a perfect strike, though it had a slight arc during flight. "I've done some pretty awesome things in my life, and this is in the top baseball events," he concluded.

Mets fan and comedian Steve Hofstetter has thrown out the first pitch before eight big league and 13 minor league games. What advice would he give to fans who may someday get the same opportunity? "Remember, you've done this before," he told me. "As Satchel Paige said, 'Just take the ball and throw strikes. Home plate doesn't move.'"

I've always said that if given the chance to throw out the first pitch, I'd like to start my delivery, stop, and do a fake first-to-third pick-off move, before returning to the stretch for the official toss home. I also thought it would be fun to send the ball to home plate like a basketball player would shoot a free throw. Not surprisingly, based on these ideas, no one has asked me to be part of their pregame ceremony, but I'm waiting and ready for when I get the call...

Go to a Playoff Game at Citi Field

Bucket Rank: 🗑️ 🗑️ 🗑️ 🗑️ 🗑️

If Opening Day is for experiencing unbridled hope and optimism and the potential for success, then postseason baseball is for feeling stress and anxiety and the potential for pain and regret. Postseason baseball in Shea Stadium provided a constant zing of tension and excitement that entered through your feet, moved up your body, and ended in your hands. It never stopped. It started before the game and continued through the final out.

I worried that Citi Field would be different, but it wasn't. It had the exact same atmosphere in 2015 as it had during October series at Shea Stadium because the building's frenetic energy doesn't come from concrete. It comes from Mets fans.

Mets players get ready for a workout prior to the 2016 wild-card game at Citi Field. (AP Images)

It got so wild with excitement at Shea Stadium that fans literally worried about the actual concrete. The second after Robin Ventura's batted ball disappeared behind the outfield wall during the bottom of the 15th inning of the 1999 National League Championship Series, I could see Shea Stadium swaying in the night. I panicked for a moment, grabbing my friend's arm for fear that it might come down.

Mets fan Tommy Dee had a similar experience seven years later at Shea Stadium after Endy Chavez robbed a home run during Game 7 of the NLCS. "He makes the catch, and we get hit with this moment of equal parts euphoria and elation mixed with terror, and I literally thought it was possible the stadium might collapse," he told me. "Of course, everything was fine, and they kept playing baseball."

Mets fans probably wish they had more experiences than they do watching postseason baseball at their home ballpark. However, despite just 18 postseason series through their first 55 years in the league, the Mets have had plenty of exhilarating moments playing October baseball, such as:

The Catch by Endy Chavez (2006 NLCS, Game 7)

The 2006 National League Championship Series came down to Game 7. In the sixth inning of a tense, back-and-forth ballgame, Mets left-fielder Endy Chavez made an acrobatic, snow-cone catch, bending his wrist over the outfield wall to rob St. Louis Cardinals third baseman Scott Rolen of a home run and keep the game tied. There was absolute silence in the air at Shea Stadium for the four seconds Rolen's ball was in flight. However, the building erupted, as did the players on the field and in the dugout, after Chavez pulled the ball from his mitt.

Bobby Jones vs. Giants (2000 NLDS, Game 4)

Mets starting pitcher Bobby Jones stole the show during Game 4 of the 2000 National League Division Series, throwing the sixth complete game, one-hitter (at the time) in postseason history. Outside of San Francisco Giants second baseman Jeff Kent's double in the fifth inning, Jones was in command the entire game. Despite going 11–6 with a 5.06 ERA during the regular season, which included a stint in the minors, Jones won Game 4 and vaulted the Mets into the National League Championship Series.

Benny Agbayani's Walk-Off Home Run (2000 NLDS, Game 3)

With the series tied 1–1, Mets outfielder and lovable fan favorite Benny Agbayani hit a walk-off home run in the 13th inning to win Game 3 of the National League Division Series against the San Francisco Giants.

Todd Pratt's Walk-Off Home Run (1999 NLDS, Game 4)

Mets All-Star catcher Mike Piazza was unable to hit as he continued to struggle with a thumb injury that had been plaguing him since summer. In the bottom of the 10th inning and the score tied during a seesaw battle with the Arizona Diamondbacks, backup catcher Todd Pratt launched a solo home run to center field that barely made it over a jumping Steve Finley. The 4–3 win sent the Mets to the National League Championship Series, where they would eventually lose to the Atlanta Braves in six games.

Mike Hampton Tosses a Complete Game (2000 NLCS, Game 5)

Mike Hampton played for the Mets just one season, but his outing in Game 5 of the National League Championship Series in 2000 cemented his place in team history. With the Mets one game away from going to the World Series, Hampton allowed three hits and struck out eight batters in a 7–0 victory that sent the Mets to the World Series for the first time in 14 years.

Tom Seaver Leads Mets to World Series (1973 NLCS, Game 5)

Tom Seaver carried the Mets into the 1973 World Series with his right arm. In Game 5 of the National League Championship Series, he pitched in and out of trouble all night but held on to send the Mets to their second World Series in five years. Immediately after the final out, hundreds and hundreds of Mets fans spilled out of the Shea Stadium stands on to the field, where they hugged and celebrated the win with their favorite players.

Lenny Dykstra's Walk-Off Home Run (1986 NLCS, Game 3)

With Mets trailing by one run in the ninth inning and on the verge of falling behind 2–1 in the 1986 National League Championship Series, Mets outfielder Lenny Dykstra scooped a low fastball into the afternoon sky that carried out of Shea Stadium and put the Mets up 2–1 in the Series.

Tommie Agee's Catch (1969 World Series, Game 3)

After leading off the game with a home run, Mets center fielder Tommie Agee made a terrific back-handed, snow-cone catch on a ball hit in the left-center gap with two men on base. His warning-track grab ended the Baltimore Orioles' rally, brought fans to their feet, and protected New York's lead.

Bill Buckner and Mookie Wilson (1986 World Series, Game 6)

With the Red Sox leading 5–3 in the 10th inning of Game 6 during the 1986 World Series and the Mets down to their final out of the season, Gary Carter, Kevin Mitchell, and Ray Knight all singled to reduce Boston's lead to one run. Bob Stanley's wild pitch to Mookie Wilson allowed the tying run to score, after which Wilson hit a slow ground ball down the first-base line. It seemed a foregone conclusion that the ball would be picked up, but instead it bounced between the legs of first baseman Bill Buckner, allowing Knight to score the winning run.

The Miracle Mets (1969 World Series, Game 5)

Thanks in large part to a two-run home run by World Series MVP Donn Clendenon and a solo home run by Al Weis, the Mets won Game 5 of the 1969 World Series in front of their home fans to secure their first world championship in franchise history.

Mets Win Second World Series (1986 World Series, Game 7)

Just as they did in Game 6, the Boston Red Sox jumped out to an early lead in Game 7, again putting the Mets on their heels. However, New York's sixth-inning rally tied the game at 3–3, after which they scored three more runs in the seventh. The Red Sox pulled to within one run, but it wasn't enough, as the Mets eventually won 8–5 for their second World Series title.

Robin Ventura's Grand Slam Single (1999 NLCS, Game 5)

In the freezing cold, rain-soaked bottom of the 15th inning of Game 5 during the 1999 National League Championship Series, Mets third baseman Robin Ventura appeared to hit a walk-off grand slam against the Atlanta Braves. However, it ended up being ruled a run-scoring single because his overzealous teammates mobbed him on field before rounding second base.

The Return to October (2015 NLDS, Game 3)

Just after the national anthem, there was a point before Game 1 of the 2015 National League Division Series started when the Citi Field public address announcer informed fans that TBS would be showing the ballpark on television for the first time and that the crowd was expected to be loud. And, *wow*, it got loud.

I was already cold from the weather, but chills went up my back after seeing all 44,000 fans on their feet, screaming, waving orange rally towels, hysterically pumped up for the first playoff game ever in Citi Field. It had been nine years since the Mets last played October baseball, and fans were clearly not taking the moment for granted. Four innings later Yoenis Cespedes hit a line-drive home run into the second deck and, though I never thought it could be possible, Citi Field got louder than it did before first pitch. It felt like another 43,000 fans made their way in to the building. Mets fans jumped on seats, hugged strangers, and ran through the aisles with banners, yelling at the top of their lungs. It was absolutely beautiful that people who might ordinarily argue about other aspects of life could bond and share a mutual experience around baseball...especially Mets postseason baseball.

Catch a T-Shirt from the Party Patrol

Bucket Rank: 🗑️ 🗑️

There are six seconds of silence following the final out of the top of the seventh inning during every Mets home game, after which Citi Field public addresser announcer, Alex Anthony, asks everyone to stand up and remove their caps for the singing of "God Bless America."

Instantly after the patriotic song ends, Anthony thanks the singer, waits for the appropriate cheers, and then invites the entire ballpark to sign along to "Take Me Out to the Ballgame."

Is it time for baseball yet? Nope, there is still time for one more song. The final note of "Take Me Out to the Ballgame" bleeds in to the beginning of "Lazy Mary," an upbeat, Italian party song recorded by Lou Monte in 1958. The song, which is mostly in Italian, is about a conversation between a mother and her daughter, who is desperately looking for a husband. To people who speak the language, its lyrics are considered overtly sexual and very risqué. However, the 95 percent of people in the stands at Citi Field—who are unable to speak Italian—do not care. The song is simply a silly, bouncy tune that is fun to dance to with friends and family.

According to a team spokesman, during the late 1990s, Brooklyn native, Italian American, and Mets closer John Franco was the first to request "Lazy Mary" be played during a game, though he didn't specify it happening in the seventh inning. That stroke of genius goes to Vito Vitiello, who has been the organization's outstanding producer of video and entertainment for more than two decades.

There are nights my daughter asks me to sing "Take Me Out to the Ballgame" to her. I do it and, as soon as I'm done singing, I feel an uncontrollable need to slide in to the bouncy, opening notes of "Lazy Mary." It's habit. It's in my DNA at this point. I have to do it.

As "Lazy Mary" blares from the Citi Field speakers, the Home Run Apple is at full attention, lights are flashing, and fans are dancing while Mr. Met and the ballpark's Party Patrol run the warning track firing T-shirts into the crowd from a potato-launcher-style plastic hand cannon.

Citi Field's Party Patrol, which was first put together by Shea Stadium in 2005, is a small group of energetic men and women in their 20s, whose sole purpose is to smile, have fun, and provide interactive entertainment on gamedays to the fans in the ballpark. Hired by the Mets, the troupe wears authentic, white home jerseys with nicknames on the back. They appear to be the happiest people in the ballpark, bouncing from section to section and task to task, which includes escorting Mr. Met, taking pictures for fans, appearing on the scoreboard, hosting contests between innings, and generally keeping everyone in a good mood.

My friend, Michelle Horsham, started working with the Party Patrol at Shea Stadium in 2006 and then moved with them to Citi Field through 2012. How do the ballparks compare?

"There isn't much of a difference between the crowds," she told me. "The layout of the seats in Shea gave us more access to them. I feel like we were able to sit with people more in between innings than at Citi. I think because it's a newer ballpark you have more people from all walks of life coming to experience what we have to offer for the first time, which was pretty awesome."

Horsham is now married in Queens, where she is a certified school counselor. She loves her current job but misses certain aspects of the Party Patrol, specifically the fans. "You see the same faces over and over, you get to know the families, their stories, and they look forward to seeing you at the games," she told me. "We also got to meet people from all over the country and the world. I miss the energy of the ballpark, the smiles on the faces of fans who've just won a prize, caught a T-shirt, or got to shake hands with Mr. Met."

I've sat in the stands and watched more than 500 Major League Baseball games. I've never caught a home run. This has never bothered me, though. I'm not really big on memorabilia. I've had the chance to reach up and catch a ball cruising to the stands, but I'm not one to dive or risk bodily harm for something I can buy at Dick's Sporting Goods. Plus, I know what a baseball feels like. I've thrown them, played catch with them, and tossed them back in to play watching practice during spring training.

However, I've always been curious about the T-shirts that are launched in to the crowd. What size are they? What's on the front of the shirt? How do they fit in to the cannon? How do they stay in that shape when hurdling through the air? I've watched thousands of them fly through the New York night but had known nothing about them.

Then, while sitting in a Loge box at Shea Stadium on Friday, September 16, 2005, during the seventh-inning stretch of a game between the Mets and Atlanta Braves, a shirt pelted me in the chest. I never saw it coming. I also won't lie; it hurt a bit. Wrapped tightly in three rubber bands, the shirt bounced off me and landed on the empty seat to my right. I had no intention of reaching for it, assuming I'd be casual and not care. But when a large man lunged from the row behind me, my instincts and reflexes took over, and I snatched it like a cat burglar from his grip.

The shirt was mine and left me with an irrational sense of accomplishment, as though I earned this trophy and deserved to bring it home. My dad, who was 55 years old at the time and sitting to my left, acted unimpressed, but I have no doubt that he was jealous.

The full seventh-inning stretch at Citi Field—start to finish—is the only five minutes in baseball that involves loud music in different languages, dancing, patriotism, apples, dead silence, loud noise, and a mascot with a baseball head firing free T-shirts at middle-aged baseball fans who push one another out of the way to get the chance to finally catch one. It's immature, fun, authentic, amateurish, and terrific. It's Citi Field in a nutshell.

. . . .

Go to Opening Day

Bucket Rank: 🗑 🗑 🗑 🗑 🗑

In my 34 years as a full-time Mets fan, I've attended 21 home Opening Days at Citi Field and Shea Stadium. I remember them all—from the hysterical parking lots to the pleasant, upbeat enthusiastic fans to the freezing cold hot chocolates. In the northeast the home opener is often a crystal clear, frigid, and windy afternoon. "The draw of Opening Day is more than just excitement for baseball's return after a long winter in the northeast," Matt Baker from Albany, New York, told me about repeatedly going to Opening Day with his friends. "It's the buzz of potential and picking up where there's unfinished business from the previous year," he said. "The team has a clean slate, and every year we think they're going to go wire-to-wire in first place."

Opening Day is about more than just the potential for success on field. It can also be a much-anticipated reunion for fans who do not keep in touch through the offseason. "My friends live all over the country. The one thing we all have is the Mets to look forward to, and Opening Day is the one day left we get to experience all together," Seth Berk from New York, New York, told me. "It is like our Thanksgiving."

Similarly, Erik Boucher from Queens uses Opening Day as a college reunion. "I meet up with the same crew every year. It's my one guaranteed trip to Citi Field every season," he explained. "It's a holiday and a reunion."

The first game each season during the final few years at Shea Stadium was always a frenzy. In part because Citi Field was being built in the distance and we knew the clock was ticking on our experiences at Shea, but it was also because the team had been winning and entered each year as a favorite to win their division.

It was the perfect mix of anxiety, hopefulness, pent-up excitement, and the need to keep moving so everyone could stay warm. This, plus expecting to get to the postseason resulted in a loud, vibrant electricity that kept fans on their feet throughout the game.

It took until 2015 to get that type of vibration out of an Opening Day crowd at Citi Field.

The ballpark's debut in 2009 had a full house and a lot of excitement, but it was actually a mild crowd. The Mets were taking the field that night for the first time since missing the previous year's postseason by again falling apart down the stretch. So, while there was an anxious feeling to get the season started there was also a fear in the air because fans were afraid they were going to end up collapsing again.

Mets fans were new to the ballpark. They had never been there before. They were slightly disoriented and wanting to finally explore all of its nooks and crannies. As a result, despite selling 41,000 tickets, there were never more than 30,000 people in their seats at a given time with the rest investigating their new home, waiting in line at Shake Shack, or kicking back in a luxurious club or suite. This continued through much of the season, creating a very low-key first year in the ballpark. It also didn't help that the Mets finished 2009 at 70–92, which kicked off a painful and tumultuous rebuilding phase that felt like it would never end.

Thankfully, that all changed in 2015.

The Mets entered the season talking proud, telling anyone that listened how they had the potential to be a postseason team. "We have high expectations," Mets manager Terry Collins told the *New York Post* just before the start of the season. "This is the year. It's time to win. We've got a good team. We've got a great clubhouse. And we're going to compete."

The Mets split their first six games of the season, all of which were on the road. Finally, they set up in Citi Field with 43,947 loud, passionate fans all eager to put wind in their sails.

The buzz in Citi Field that afternoon was like nothing I had experienced the previous 10 years, including even 2007, when fans were still excited but apprehensive after losing so dramatically to the St. Louis Cardinals to end the 2006 National League Championship Series.

The crowd in Citi Field had been electric before 2015, specifically at the All-Star Game, on Matt Harvey Day, Johan Santana's no-hitter, and throughout the Summer of Dickey. The difference between those games and the 2015 home opener was that—for the first time—every single fan was focused on and optimistic about the entire team on field.

They weren't just excited about a new building, one specific guy, a unique event, or one performance. Finally, we were all excited about the Mets and what could be in store after the remaining 155 games. "The crowd brought it," David Wright told SNY after the game. "They were electric," Daniel Murphy added. "There was buzz in the stands."

Darryl Strawberry once told me this push-and-pull relationship with Mets fans is what he missed most when he left for Los Angeles to play for the Dodgers. And it's a big reason why he struggled to find consistent success after leaving the Mets. He said he missed the love, but he also missed the "tough love," which provided motivation that he didn't realize he was missing until he was gone.

The power that fans can have is evident in Strawberry's quote. But it's also palpable when at a game. The thing about Opening Day, though, which is not the case during every game that follows, is that there's a justifiable feeling of hope in the air that no one can shoot down.

Hope is felt in the way people are patient in line. It's heard when they speak. It's seen when they refrain from booing a botched moment and replace it instead with, "That's okay, you'll get 'em next time."

Opening Day is an optimistic place, the perfect bridge between spring and summer.

It's my favorite day of the year. "To me, Opening Day represents a fresh start to a new year," Michael Goldberg from Massapequa, New York, told me about his experiences going to Opening Day with his 20-year-old son. "No matter how bad it was the season before, there is always hope on Opening Day. I love the atmosphere and seeing all the parent-child relationships and traditions that are carried out year after year."

My mom, Maryjane, is responsible for taking me on hard-core, impromptu trips to Shea Stadium during the season, all of which sparked my love of baseball and the Mets. However, it was my dad, Michael, who was my wing-man on Opening Day. In time thanks to tailgates and hanging with me during games, he became friends with hundreds of Mets fans, be it online through #MetsTwitter or The 7 Line Army.

In 2009 I was able to get him a media pass to watch batting practice on the field on Opening Day, which would be the ballpark's first game ever. Obviously, he and I were there early. We stood next to one another—as father and son—just to the left of home plate with grass and dirt beneath us. While gazing under the blue sky at the magnificent new building, an old voice behind us said, "Excuse me, can you unlock this door?"

When, Where, and How Much

WHEN: Home opener for 2017 is April 3, 2017, and the game time is 1:10.

WHERE: Citi Field is located at 123-01 Roosevelt Avenue Flushing, New York, 11368.

COST: $50 to $760, according to the Mets website.

Taking a picture, I didn't immediately turn around, but my dad did. I looked over, and he was talking to Fred Wilpon and Saul Katz, the team's principal owners and the men who had a major hand in building Citi Field. "I seemed to have forgotten my key," Wilpon said, smiling behind a backstop door that was being held shut by a plastic zip tie.

Realizing these two men, who own the ballpark, couldn't get on field, my dad reached in to his Indiana Jones-inspired satchel resting off his right shoulder and dug out a Swiss army knife, which never should have been allowed to have on the premises. As expected, he started sawing through the zip tie. Everything about this seemed wrong and weird. So fearing for my job, I asked Mr. Wilpon if what my dad was doing was okay. "Son," he said, smiling, "I own the place, it's fine."

It took less than a minute for my dad to saw them through, after which the two owners stepped on to *their* field. My dad and I attended nine Opening Days; each one is my favorite memory. In May of 2016, my dad passed away after a sudden and aggressive battle with lung cancer. He wrote this poem in 2010, which I plan to read before every Opening Day.

Opening Day for Baseball!

It's leather and laces and chalk lines on bases.

The smell of beer in the breezes,

it triggers an image that freezes,

in your memory from a time when you were small,

on another day just like today...

It's Opening Day for Baseball!

Fathers and sons filling up stadiums.

From New York to L.A. on Opening Day,

we'll pencil in names of our heroes,

who's stats, today, all start from zero.

We'll record them all for the days that'll come.

It's Opening Day for Baseball!

We'll cheer and we'll eat, we'll stand up from our seats.

We'll high-five and we'll yell,

at players and umps and venders who sell,

all the ingredients that add to the day.

It's Opening Day for Baseball!

There'll be loser and winners, old timers and beginners,

both on the field and in the stands.

We're here cause in our hearts we're all fans,

of the game and the experiences we take home.

It's Opening Day for Baseball!

—Michael Cerrone, April 2010

Be Terrific Like Tom Seaver

Bucket Rank: 🗑️ 🗑️ 🗑️ 🗑️ 🗑️

Tom Seaver made his big league debut with the Mets in 1967 and quickly became the organization's first superstar. He went on to win 198 games for New York, helped them win their first world championship in 1969, had his number retired, and now represents them in the Hall of Fame. He's simply "Tom Terrific" and aptly referred to as, "the Franchise," since he essentially put the Mets on baseball's map.

Seaver's Mets legacy is unmatched. He is the greatest pitcher to ever wear their uniform and the organization's most accomplished homegrown player. However, it almost never happened, as he was drafted by two different teams prior to joining the Mets. After serving in the United States Marine Corps Reserves for six months of active duty in the reserves, Seaver was drafted by the Los Angeles Dodgers during June of 1965. He demanded a $70,000 signing bonus, which was unprecedented at that time in baseball. The Dodgers refused to give him the money so he returned to pitching for the University of Southern California and legendary Trojans coach Rod Dedeaux.

The following June, Seaver was selected by the Atlanta Braves, who signed him to a $40,000 deal. For all intents and purposes, Seaver was a member of the Braves before the Mets. However, according to Major League Baseball rules during the mid-1960s, teams could not negotiate or sign a player after the start of the college season. And so because the University of Southern California had already played two exhibition games between the time of the draft and his signing, then-MLB commissioner William Eckert voided the contract despite Seaver never playing in either game.

Seaver decided to again return to USC, figuring he would get a third shot at joining an MLB team the following year. His plan was stopped, though, when the NCAA revoked his amateur status because he technically signed a big league contract, which made him ineligible for the next year's MLB draft.

In a unique ruling, Eckert decided that all MLB teams could match Atlanta's offer to Seaver. The Cleveland Indians, Philadelphia Phillies, and Mets all stepped up, at which point Eckert put their names in a lottery to determine who would win the rights to negotiate. Thankfully, the Mets won, signed him to a $51,000 contract, and the rest was history.

Seaver spent 1966 pitching for the Triple A Jacksonville Suns. It was his only year in the minor leagues, during which he was 12–12 with a 3.13 ERA while striking out 188 batters in 210 innings. He joined the big league Mets the next year and made an immediate impact. In his first season, Seaver won 16 games, struck out 170 batters, had a 2.76 ERA, and was voted Rookie of the Year. Prior to his promotion, the Mets had a .322 winning percentage through five seasons and never finished better than last place. In 1968 and 1969, which were Seaver's second and third seasons in the big leagues, the Mets had a .534 winning percentage and won their first World Series.

In 1969 Seaver won the first of his eventual three Cy Young Awards after winning 25 games, posting a 2.21 ERA, throwing 18 complete games and five shutouts, and striking out 208 batters. Incredibly, his best work on a pitcher's mound was yet to come.

The following year, on April 22, 1970, at Shea Stadium, Seaver set an MLB record by striking out the last 10 batters of a game. In the top of the sixth inning, San Diego Padres outfielder Cito Gaston lined out to right field, after which his teammates never put another ball in play. Seaver finished the game with 19 strikeouts. No pitcher in baseball before or since has struck out 10 consecutive batters in a game.

Seaver had his second best season totals in 1971, when—at 26 years old—he went 20–10 with a career-best 1.76 ERA and 289 strikeouts.

Unfortunately, he finished second in Cy Young voting to legendary Chicago Cubs right-hander Fergie Jenkins. Seaver had a breathtaking stat line, possibly the best of his career, though some fans argue what he did two years later had a bigger impact on the team.

In mid-August of 1973, the Mets were in last place and 12 games below .500 but just seven and a half games out of first place. From that point forward, the Mets won 29 of their final 43 games to win the NL East, though they eventually lost to the Oakland A's in the World Series. Seaver ended the year 19–10, one win short of his third consecutive 20-win season. However, because he had the league's best ERA (2.08), most complete games (18), most strikeouts (251), lowest WHIP (a Walks and Hits Per Innings Pitched of 0.976), and the best strikeout-to-walk ratio (3.92), he deservedly won his second Cy Young Award and finished eighth in the league's MVP voting. According to BaseballReference.com, Seaver's 10.6 WAR (Wins Above Replacement) in 1973 was the highest of any single season during his career. Dwight Gooden's 13.3 in 1985 was the only higher total by a Mets pitcher.

At 30 years old and in his ninth big league season in 1975, Seaver won his final Cy Young Award, the result of his fourth consecutive 20-win season. It was also his last elite season. To the surprise and dismay of most Mets fans, Seaver was traded to the Cincinnati Reds in 1977. And just as they did before he arrived to the big leagues, the Mets finished in last place the next three years.

Seaver pitched well for the Reds, for whom he threw his only no-hitter in 1978. (He had five one-hitters with the Mets.) In 1982 he was traded back to the Mets. Unfortunately for nostalgic Mets fans, Seaver was left unprotected during the free-agent compensation draft of 1984 and selected by the Chicago White Sox where he would remain until he was traded to the Boston Red Sox in 1986. He did not get to play against the Mets in the 1986 World Series because he struggled to return in time from an injury.

Seaver retired the next season in 1987, ending his career 311–205 with 3,640 strikeouts, a 2.86 ERA, 61 shutouts, and a major league record of at least 200 strikeouts in nine consecutive seasons. In 1992 Seaver was voted into the baseball Hall of Fame with the highest percentage of votes ever at the time, appearing on 98.84 percent of the ballots. Despite not pitching for the Mets in more than 30 years, he has still thrown the most innings in franchise history (3,045). He's also first in wins (198), ERA (2.57), strikeouts (2,541), complete games (171), shutouts (44), and games started by a Mets pitcher (395).

It's difficult to imagine how life might have been for the Mets had the Dodgers been able to sign him out of high school. Or had the Braves not violated a rule when drafting him the next summer. Or had the Mets not lucked out beating the Indians and Phillies for the right to sign him out of college. Instead "Tom Terrific" joined the Mets and remains the best player to ever wear their uniform.

Enjoy Some New York-Style Piazza

Bucket Rank: 🗑️ 🗑️ 🗑️ 🗑️

During a lunch break when working customer service at Home Depot on May 22, 1998, I answered a persistent phone call from my mother. "Did you hear?" She started, sounding overly excited. "The Mets traded for that pizza guy!"

I laughed, though I knew exactly who she was referring to. Mike Piazza was selected by the Los Angeles Dodgers with their last pick during the 1988 MLB Amateur Draft. It was the same year the

Dodgers stunned New York by beating the Mets in seven games during the National League Championship Series.

Piazza's dad, Vince, who once built his son an indoor batting cage, lobbied his friend, Dodgers manager Tommy Lasorda, to have his team draft Mike. "The Dodgers didn't want him," Lasorda told *USA TODAY*. "Nobody wanted him. I kept telling our guys, 'I want him drafted. I don't care where or when, but draft him.' So they draft him."

However, because he was their 62nd selection that season, and essentially a courtesy pick for Lasorda, the Dodgers didn't reach out to Piazza until late summer. According to Lasorda, the Dodgers had no intention of keeping him, though they were impressed with his ability to hit. So an impromptu Lasorda said Piazza could be a catcher, not a first baseman, which got the Dodgers to sigh him to their basic $15,000 contract. The only problem was that Piazza wasn't a catcher. Lasorda made it up, knowing it was the only way his team would give his friend's son a chance. So, Piazza caught a flight to the Dominican Republic, where at 20 years old and the first American player to ever be in that camp, he worked out at the organization's training facility to learn how to be a backstop. "You have no idea what this kid went through," Lasorda told *USA TODAY*. "They never wanted him. They held it against him because of my relationship with him. They wanted to break him."

Piazza nearly quit the next summer at Single A Vero Beach in Florida, where he struggled to learn his position and found himself in confrontations with the team's coaching staff, who resented that he was drafted because of his relationship with Lasorda. "It was a difficult time, but it helped get me to where I needed to be," Piazza told me during an interview at Tradition Field in 2016. "It made me stronger, mentally and physically, and taught me how to be patient."

Piazza made his major league debut in 1992. The next season he made the All-Star team as a catcher and won the National League's Rookie of the Year Award four years after first putting a mask on. By 1997 he was widely considered the best hitting catcher in baseball and on his way to becoming the greatest hitting catcher of all time. He hit .362 that season with 40 home runs and 124 RBIs while finishing second in voting for the NL Most Valuable Player Award. It would be his last full year in Dodger blue.

The next spring, with less than a year to go before being a free agent, Piazza was traded to the Florida Marlins. He had been reportedly on the trade block since rejecting an $84 million contract offer from the Dodgers, and the Mets were among teams that were showing interest in acquiring him. So, it was a shock to baseball when he ended up in Miami, where the Marlins were 15 games below .500, in last place, and in the process of dismantling their team—not rebuilding it—after a World Series run the year before.

The Mets had the National League's worst winning percentage from 1993 to 1996. However, after hiring Bobby Valentine in 1997, they surprised Mets fans by winning 88 games and chasing the wild-card deep in to September. Immediately after winning the World Series, the Marlins began trading away their most expensive players, including sending pitchers Al Leiter and reliever Dennis Cook to the Mets. So, the next season, when the Marlins acquired Piazza with the intent of flipping him for prospects, it made sense to phone the Mets again since both organizations were quite familiar with one another's farm system. "Piazza was a marquee-type guy, and we needed that type of player," then-general manager Steve Phillips told me in 2015 about the decision to pursue Piazza. "We were a good little team, but we needed to get a superstar. At the same time, we know from previous discussions that the Marlins liked our top outfield prospect, Preston Wilson, as well as some of our young pitching talent."

The opportunity for the Mets to acquire Piazza was in place, the prospects needed were available, the front office was ready to make a deal, and the team's fans certainly were hungry for something to get done. However, ownership still needed to sign off on the acquisition, knowing Piazza would be a free agent seeking a multi-year, record-setting contract the next winter. "The legend that has built up around the trade is that Nelson Doubleday wanted to do the deal, and Wilpon did not, but that public pressure, particularly from WFAN's radio hosts Mike Francesa and Chris Russo, moved Wilpon to change his mind," *New York Post* columnist Joel Sherman wrote in 2016.

According to Sherman, five former members of the 1998 front office confirmed to him that Wilpon needed to be convinced. "Fred loves prospects and he really loved our pitching prospects," an anonymous source from the 1998 staff told him. "He was frustrated by what happened with Generation K—actually, we all were—and I don't think he wanted to send our remaining top pitching prospects to a division rival for a guy that might leave as a free agent in six months. It was a fair concern, but Phillips, Doubleday, Dave Howard, even Bobby Valentine, all helped to change his mind. And thank God they did."

Finally, seven days after leaving Los Angeles for Miami, the Marlins traded Piazza to the Mets for Wilson and pitching prospects Geoff Geotz and Ed Yarnall. "I think we invented the chest bump," Phillips said, when I asked him in 2015 how he reacted after completing the deal to bring Piazza to the Mets. "It was so exciting, especially knowing we were about to make an announcement that was going to rock New York City."

In his first game with the Mets on May 23, 1998, Piazza hit an RBI double through the right-center field gap. It gave the Mets a 2–0 lead as they went on to defeat the Milwaukee Brewers 3–0. "I'm on cloud nine right now, but I need some sleep," Piazza told New York reporters after the game, which was totally understandable considering his three-team, four-city tour during the previous eight days.

Piazza immediately begin hitting with the Mets, though it took him time to find his power stroke at Shea Stadium. He was frequently booed in June and early July for struggling at home and not hitting in the clutch. However, after announcing that he wanted to postpone contract talks with the Mets until after the season, Piazza got hot at the plate in August and never looked back. "It was a little stressful for a while," Phillips admitted to me about the early going of Piazza's time in a Mets uniform. "But once it clicked, and when the fans accepted Piazza, it became everything we thought it could be."

In his 106 games with the Mets that season, Piazza hit .348 with a .419 on-base percentage, 23 home runs, 33 doubles, and 76 RBIs. Unfortunately, despite a spike in attendance, the Mets actually played slightly worse baseball than they did before Piazza was acquired and they ended up missing the postseason by just one and a half games.

The season ended with no postseason and Piazza eligible to be a free agent, leaving Mets fans to wonder whether his time in New York would be reduced to just four months. "It had been going so well and the way we hoped it would, and so we felt there was a chance we could bring him back," Phillips told me, though he admitted to also being nervous in advance of restarting negotiations.

Thankfully, it took just four days for the two sides to agree on a seven-year, $91 million deal, which included a limited no-trade clause, making it the most lucrative contract in baseball history at the time. "This tells the fans that we appreciate the fact that they came back to watch us play after we acquired Mike," Doubleday said the day the deal was announced. "They wanted a marquee player, we needed a marquee player, and we got them a marquee player."

The Mets became Piazza's team in 1999, during which the franchise returned to the postseason for the first time in 11 years. The Mets got back to the postseason in 2000, marking the first ever back-to-back postseason appearance in franchise history. In 2000 Piazza and the Mets won the National League pennant and advanced to the World Series to face the cross-town rival Yankees, who were in the midst of a dynastic run of championships.

Earlier that season, during a regular-season game against the Yankees, pitcher Roger Clemens hit Piazza in the head with a fastball. Piazza was knocked to the ground where he lay on his back, bleeding and seemingly unconscious for several minutes. The incident resulted in a concussion and forced Piazza to miss the All-Star Game. It also made Clemens an enemy of Mets fans, who continue to insist the pitch was intentional. Piazza entered the game having had consistent success against Clemens, who was known around baseball as someone who intimidated hitters by throwing inside fastballs.

In the World Series, all eyes were on Clemens and Piazza during Game 1. In their first battle since Piazza was hit in the head, Clemens threw a pitch that broke Piazza's bat as the ball rolled in to foul territory. However, a jagged end of Piazza's bat barrel snapped off and flew directly at Clemens, who caught it and threw it at Piazza, who was jogging slowly up the first-base line. The crowd at Yankee Stadium jumped to its feet, instantly turning a baseball game into what felt like a steel-cage match. Instead of returning to the batter's box, Piazza slowly walked toward the mound and glared at Clemens, who looked completely confused. "I thought it was the ball," Clemens can be seen saying to the first-base umpire, which still makes absolutely zero sense. *Okay, let's say he did think it was the ball, then why was throwing at Piazza?* Nevertheless, Clemens kept repeating his question, going so far as to ask for a new ball despite having one in his hand. In standard baseball fashion, both benches cleared and met at the mound. Words were exchanged, but no punches were thrown, and, thankfully, nobody was ejected.

The Mets went on to lose the World Series. However, four years later, Piazza was forced to catch Clemens during the 2004 All-Star Game. Clemens gave up six runs in the first inning. And though no one will admit it, I like to believe Piazza let each opposing batter know what was about to be thrown so Clemens would look like a fool on national television.

Piazza's most important moment with the Mets had less to do with baseball and more to do with lifting spirits, distracting New York, and giving people a moment to smile. Ten days after the September 11 terrorist attacks, baseball returned to New York City as the Mets welcomed the Atlanta Braves to Shea Stadium. It was an awkward, sad, and somber evening, as everyone involved walked the emotional line between what was appropriate and what was necessary. However, in the eighth inning and with the Mets struggling to remain in a playoff race, Piazza hit a game-changing, two-run home run off Braves reliever Steve Karsay. The Shea Stadium crowd went wild, chanting "USA! USA!" "It was almost like a blur to me. It was almost like a dream, sort of surreal," Piazza said after the game. "I'm just so happy I gave the people something to cheer. There was a lot of emotion. It was just a surreal sort of energy out there."

The Mets struggled in the years after losing to the Yankees in the World Series, during which Piazza's production dropped as his injuries and age started to rise. In 2004 at 35 years old, Piazza was asked to split his time between catching and playing first base. He looked terribly awkward, and the experiment was abandoned before the next season. Sadly, on October 2, 2005, Piazza played his final game with the Mets, as it was reported that he and the team planned to part ways after the season. During the game Mets manager Willie Randolph replaced Piazza after the eighth inning, so the 47,718 fans in Shea Stadium could give him one last cheer. Piazza bowed toward the stands, blowing kisses to fans around the stadium before slowly jogging down the dugout steps. He played the next season with the San Diego Padres and then signed on to be a designated hitter for the Oakland A's. Piazza retired after the 2007 season with 427 home runs, the most ever hit by a catcher.

In 2013 the Mets inducted Piazza into their Hall of Fame. And in 2016, after he was finally elected to the Baseball Hall of Fame with their hat on, the Mets retired his No. 31. He is only the second player, along with Tom Seaver's No. 41, to have his number retired by the Mets. "They never should have traded him," Lasorda said. "They made the biggest mistake of their lives. But look who got the last laugh, and now the rest is history."

In the end Piazza played 16 years, half of them for the Mets, and most all of them were behind the plate. He hit .308 for his career, made the All-Star team 12 times, and played in eight postseason series, including five with the Mets.

Chapter 3

Places to Go

Visit Cooperstown

Bucket Rank: 🗑 🗑 🗑

D uring the summer of 2016, Mike Piazza joined Tom Seaver as the only players in the National Baseball Hall of Fame who wear a Mets hat on their honorary plaque. Located in Cooperstown, New York, roughly 200 miles from Citi Field, the National Baseball Museum is open seven days a week, though closed on Thanksgiving, Christmas, and New Year's Day. At the tune of $70 for a family of four, it serves as the historical center of baseball in the United States and is filled with baseball-related artifacts, exhibits, and memorabilia.

My personal favorites include a 1889 silver-plated season pass for the Polo Grounds, the ball and cap from Don Larsen's perfect game during the 1956 World Series, and Rickey Henderson's neon green batting gloves from when he stole his 939th base.

The National Baseball Hall of Fame also recently opened a 9/11 exhibit that pays tribute to baseball's role in New York during the aftermath of the terrorist attacks in 2001. The breathtaking exhibit includes Piazza's jersey from September 21, 2001, during which he hit a dramatic and memorable home run in the eighth inning at Shea Stadium. The display also included a baseball found in the rubble of the World Trade Center, a NYPD hat worn by Mets manager Bobby Valentine, the FDNY hat worn by Mets relief pitcher John Franco, and a ticket stub from the game scheduled for September 11 at Yankee Stadium.

In addition to being a mecca for baseball, Cooperstown is also a charming, little New York town, featuring tons of culture, history, outdoor activities, restaurants, ice cream shops, and more. The Hall of

Fame's focal point is its Plaque Gallery, which acknowledges the 317 people to ever participate in baseball.

Seaver's 98.84 percentage of votes was the highest total until Ken Griffey Jr.'s 2016 percentage of 99.32 edged him. Inducted in 1992, Seaver received 425 of a possible 430 votes during his first year of eligibility. "Three voters submitted blank ballots in protest of Pete Rose [for not being on the ballot]," Jeff Idelson, Hall of Fame vice president of communications and education, told *USA TODAY* in 2006. "Another, following open-heart surgery overlooked Seaver after filling out his ballot, and a fifth said he didn't vote for first-time eligibles."

Piazza, who was my favorite player of his era, was inducted in 2016 and received 365 of 440 votes. He was first on the ballot in 2013, when he received just 57.8 percent. He remained 28 votes shy of the

The National Baseball Hall of Fame showcases its Mike Piazza display when the catcher was inducted in 2016. (USA TODAY Sports Images)

When, Where, and How Much

WHEN: Regular hours are 9:00 AM to 5:00 PM. Summer hours are 9:00 AM to 9:00 PM. It's open seven days a week but closed on Thanksgiving, Christmas, and New Year's Day.

WHERE: 25 Main Street, Cooperstown, New York, 13326.

COST: It is free for museum members, active/retired career military, and children six or under; $23 for adults (13 to 64); $15 for seniors (65 and over); $12 for veterans; and $12 for children (seven to 12).

necessary 75 percent two years later before finally getting over the hump in 2016.

Cooperstown is also home to Doubleday Field, named for Abner Doubleday and located two blocks from the National Baseball Hall of Fame and Museum. The legendary ballpark typically hosts more than 350 baseball games every year, ranging from youth baseball to high school and collegiate tournaments to senior leagues.

I pitched on this field during a Babe Ruth League All-Star tournament in July of 1990. And, though I can't prove it, I'm pretty sure I gave up the biggest home run that field has ever seen. The hit ball sailed through the sky and broke a shutter on the small white house beyond the right-field wall.

Seaver and Piazza may be the only Mets players in the National Baseball Hall of Fame who wear a Mets hat on their honorary plaque. However, the inductee's plaque lists every organization he played for in equal font size. So in addition to Seaver and Piazza, you will also notice Roberto Alomar, Richie Ashburn, Yogi Berra, Gary Carter, Tom Glavine, Rickey Henderson, Pedro Martinez, Eddie Murray, Nolan Ryan, Duke Snider, Warren Spahn, Casey Stengel, Joe Torre, and George Weiss, all of whom wear a different team's cap on their plaque, but who are all listed in connection to the Mets.

In time, I expect Carlos Beltran to enter the Hall of Fame also wearing a Mets hat. The fact is, he played more games for the Mets than he did with any other team, while also having his most success and putting up some of his best statistics. In the end Beltran is one of just five players to hit 500 doubles, 400 home runs, and steal 300 bases, while winning three Gold Glove Awards. He should get in, and—when he does—he should be wearing blue and orange like Piazza and Seaver.

Go to a Brooklyn Cyclones Game

Bucket Rank:

The Brooklyn Cyclones are a minor league baseball team based in Brooklyn, New York. They play in the short-season A classification of the New York–Penn League. They are owned by Fred Wilpon's Sterling Equities, the majority owner of the New York Mets, with whom the Cyclones are affiliated.

The Cyclones play their games at MCU Park, located just off the legendary Coney Island boardwalk in Brooklyn. Tickets are inexpensive. It'll cost roughly $20 to sit in the front row behind home plate. And, if you go to games on Wednesday, every ticket—even the best seats in the house—is $10.

Personally, I prefer the bleacher seats. There is something about eating a Nathan's hot dog, sitting in the bleachers, and watching a ballgame in Brooklyn that feels nostalgic and appropriate. As a Mets fan, I feel a connection to the Brooklyn Dodgers and New York Giants—since my favorite team was essentially born out of their departures to the West Coast. In fact, the interlocking NY and the team's colors are an homage to what the Dodgers and Giants left behind.

Prior to the Cyclones, Brooklyn had not hosted a professional baseball team since the Dodgers left Ebbets Field for Los Angeles, California, in 1958. In 1999 New York mayor Rudolph Giuliani announced a deal that would bring a minor league affiliate for the Yankees to Staten Island and a minor league affiliate for the Mets to Brooklyn.

Prior to the 2000 season, Sterling purchased the St. Catharines Stompers from Ontario, Canada, renamed them Queens Kings, and temporarily moved them to St. John's University, where they continued to be affiliated with the Toronto Blue Jays. The next season, with new players, new uniforms, a new affiliation, and a new name, they began play at KeySpan Park. In honor of the Coney Island Cyclone roller coaster at nearby Astroland amusement park, the team was named "Cyclones," which was the top entry from an open fan vote.

In 2010 Municipal Credit Union took over naming rights from KeySpan, changing the stadium's name to MCU Park. According to most people who regularly go to games, the seats along the third-base line are fun because they also offer the best view of the Parachute Jump, which is the 250-foot tall, now-defunct amusement ride whose open-frame steel structure remains a Coney Island landmark. However, because they're not blocked by stadium netting, sections 15, 16, and 17 along the visitor's dugout will get you the best overall view, including a perfect shot of the Thunderbolt, the classic-looking, 125-foot tall roller coaster built in 2014.

The truth is, though, every seat at MCU Park is great, especially since it's only 20 rows deep.

Cyclones games are always entertaining and sometimes sort of silly. But silly in a youthful, get-over-yourself, and enjoy-the-moment kind of way. Kids always have a great time.

The team and ballpark are known in the area for their outrageous and unique theme nights, which is usually the case for most minor league affiliates. In the last year, they've had a Seinfeld Night (with a Mets-themed Jerry Seinfeld bobblehead giveaway) and Star Wars Night that included Darth Vader and a collection of Stormtroopers. MCU Park and the Cyclones also do an outstanding job honoring local communities and service people, specifically the DSNY, FDNY, and NYPD.

The Cyclones also have an entertaining 12-woman dance team called, "Dem Bums," which is how most critics referred to the Brooklyn Dodgers back in the day. They're not difficult to find since they're always in view dancing, bouncing, hopping, and engaging with the crowd from the field, bleachers, and on top of the home dugout.

With all due respect to the "Bums," the real star at MCU Park is Sandy the Seagull. The team's mascot since their inception was named after former Dodgers great Sandy Koufax. In addition to enjoying the standard mascot antics of firing T-shirt cannons, posing for pictures, and dancing with fans, kids seem to love most the chance to race him around the bases at the end of every game.

In 12 years writing about baseball, I have been to 12 minor league ballparks, and MCU Park easily has the best food. I'm not daring, I'm pretty tame, but I've seen things served in other parks that would make you fast for a week. In Brooklyn you'll find Bushwick's Arancini Brosh, which makes six different types of rice balls served in small egg cartons, the most expensive of which are just $10. Their Nutella ball, which is soaked in milk, sugar, and cinnamon, is a delicacy.

Just like at Citi Field, MCU Park features Pig Guy NYC's bacon-on-a-stick. There's also a Tacos El Tigre if you want really good, spicy pork

When, Where, and How Much

WHEN: Regular season runs from June until September.

WHERE: MCU Park, 1904 Surf Avenue, Brooklyn, New York, 11224.

COST OF TICKETS: Average ticket cost is about $10.

COST OF FOOD: $15 should cover a meal and dessert. Nathan's ranges between $4 to $6. Burgers are about $6. Arancini Bros has rice balls (three for $6 and six for $10), and Pig Guy NYC's has various pork options. The signature Cyclones hot dog—a Chorizo dog, pretzel bun with provolone, pulled pork, and bacon from Pig Guy—is $14.

COST OF DRINKS: Coors and Coors Light are $7.75. Draft options are slightly more expensive.

tacos; Cool Supplier's ice pops; Nathan's famous hot dogs; and my Citi Field favorite, Premio sausage, peppers, and onion grinder. "Hot dogs are as much a part of Coney Island as the beach, roller coasters, and boardwalk," said Cyclones vice president Steve Cohen. "When we were coming up with an identity for our team back in 2001, one of the names that we strongly considered was the Hot Dogs."

Once you have ordered your food, taken in the view, checked out "Dem Bums," and high-fived Sandy the Seagull, it's time to watch some baseball. Admittedly, they're not the best baseball players in the world, but one day they might be. Brooklyn is typically where the Mets send their most recent draft class to begin their professional careers, and in some cases, there are guys here that were in high school or college just a month or two earlier. However, they all hustle, appreciate the fans, sign autographs, smile, and clearly value the experience of beginning their baseball lives in New York.

And in some cases, Brooklyn's manager is more the star of the show than the players.

During their first season ever, the Cyclones finished 52–24, which represented the best record in their league. They were managed by Edgar Alfonzo, the brother of Edgardo Alfonzo, who was a fan favorite as the Mets' third and second baseman during the late '90s. In time Edgardo would also manage the Cyclones as did other former Mets players Howard Johnson (2002), Tim Teufel (2003), Mookie Wilson (2005), and Wally Backnan (2010).

The first Cyclones player to get to the big leagues was infielder Danny Garcia, who made his debut with the Mets on September 2, 2003, at Shea Stadium. In his wake the Cyclones have promoted 60 of the franchise's more than 500 players to the major leagues. Cyclones alumni Michael Conforto, Lucas Duda, Wilmer Flores, Juan Lagares, Seth Lugo, Rafael Montero, Brandon Nimmo, Kevin Plawecki, T.J. Rivera, Hansel Robles, and Gabriel Ynoa all spent time on the Mets big league roster in 2016.

Also in 2016, after serving a suspension that kept him off field for nine months, hometown favorite Jose Reyes suited up for the Cyclones after rejoining the organization as a free agent in June. The Cyclones said they sold 2,500 tickets in 24 hours after the Mets announced Reyes would make his return to baseball in Brooklyn.

Obviously, the Brooklyn team's main rival is the Staten Island Yankees, who are affiliated with the New York Yankees and located just 11 miles away. The two teams have the closest proximity of any two affiliates in the minor leagues. According to the two teams, they generally sell out both stadiums any time they play each other in what is often called the "Ferry Series," "Battle of the Burroughs," or, "Battle of the Bridges."

Located on the first-base side of the Jackie Robinson Rotunda at Citi Field, the Mets Hall of Fame and Museum is definitely worth checking out. (AP Images)

. . . .

Tour the Mets Hall of Fame and Museum

Bucket Rank: 🗑 🗑 🗑

The Mets Hall of Fame and Museum is a wonderful walk down memory lane. Located in Citi Field on the first-base side of the Jackie Robinson Rotunda, the 3,700-square-foot memorial features artifacts, interactive displays, and highlight videos celebrating the franchise's biggest accomplishments. The museum's doors are open during all of Citi Field home games and is accessible to fans with a ticket to that day's game.

The Hall of Fame and museum didn't exist when Citi Field first opened in 2009. The Shea Stadium version had been located in the exclusive Diamond Club, leaving the majority of fans unable to access it. I was told the Mets initially planned to relocate the museum to center field when moving to their new ballpark. However, production was held up due in part to a less-than-ideal fit for foot traffic but also because of security specifications set forth by the National Baseball Hall of Fame and Populous, the architect and design firm tasked with its development. The Mets Hall of Fame and Museum eventually debuted the next season in its current location, which is spacious, prominent, and perfectly situated for fans entering the ballpark. "We had talked about a museum for a long time," the team's senior director of marketing Tina Mannix told Bleacher Report in 2010. "It was something that had been part of the conversation and it was really just a matter of priorities and finding the right space and allocating the right amount of time to do it the right way."

The majority of the items in the team's museum are on loan from their archives, the National Baseball Hall of Fame, and a go-to group of private collectors, such as Mets fan Robert Brender, who let the team display his 1987 game-worn Darryl Strawberry home jersey, among other items. "As someone who was heavy into collecting game-used memorabilia, specifically Mets game-used jerseys, the most satisfying feeling was being able to have other fans of the team see those items and appreciate them," Brender told me. "Most collectors have small displays at their homes to dress up a sports room, but very few have items rare enough to be in a museum. To have thousands, maybe millions, of fans see them, it was validating as a collector."

In addition to countless game-worn jerseys, the museum has displayed hundreds of incredible artifacts, including one of Keith Hernandez's 11 Gold Gloves, Tom Seaver's Cy Young Award, an original record of "Meet the Mets," John Franco's FDNY cap that he wore after 9/11, the actual baseball Mookie Wilson hit between Bill Buckner's legs, a variety of championship rings, pennants, and even road-trip luggage tags.

Obviously, the 1969 and 1986 World Series trophies are must-see pieces of memorabilia. They will each give you chills. However, my favorite item will always be the original hand-written scouting report for a then-17-year-old Darryl Strawberry, which was discovered years later in the organization's human resource department. According to the 1979 report, Strawberry is listed as a "below-average hitter" worth roughly $60,000 with the potential to be an above-average power hitter with an accurate, strong arm.

The team's Hall of Fame is designed to recognize the careers of former players, managers, broadcasters, and executives. An exclusive panel that includes legendary reporter Marty Noble, public relations director Jay Horwitz, broadcasters Gary Cohen and Howie Rose, Jeff Wilpon, and other team executives makes its decisions.

The 27 inductees honored with plaques in the Museum at Citi Field are Joan Payson, Casey Stengel (1981), Gil Hodges, George Weiss (1982), Johnny Murphy, Bill Shea (1983), Ralph Kiner, Bob Murphy, Lindsey Nelson (1984), Bud Harrelson, Rusty Staub (1986), Tom Seaver (1988), Jerry Koosman (1989), Ed Kranepool (1990), Cleon Jones (1991), Jerry Grote (1992), Tug McGraw (1993), Mookie Wilson (1996), Keith Hernandez (1997), Gary Carter (2001), Tommie Agee (2002), Frank Cashen, Dwight Gooden, Davey Johnson, Darryl Strawberry (2010), John Franco (2012), and Mike Piazza (2013).

Meet a Friend at the Apple

Bucket Rank: 🗑️ 🗑️

The Home Run Apple outside Citi Field, between lots F and G, is an easy and iconic location to meet up with friends and family before a game. It's also another great reminder of Shea Stadium. The gigantic, new apple inside the ballpark, which hides in center field, waiting to emerge after a home run, is 4,800 pounds and 16½ feet tall, according to the team. The one outside Citi Field, which is the original Home Run Apple from Shea Stadium, is half the size and weighs roughly 400 pounds.

Just like the current apple in Citi Field, the old apple has a Mets logo on its front and a flat, bent green stem and leaf poking out its top. The current in-stadium apple rises out of a massive canister, while the old one ascended from a 10-foot-tall black plywood top hat. The Shea apple outside Citi Field now features a more sturdy, well-constructed hat capable of withstanding the elements and the occasional fan abuse. "The Home Run Apple, which has a quirky following all its own, dovetails perfectly with the frequently wacky, often kitschy, sporadically glorious history of the Mets," Johnette Howard wrote for ESPN.com in 2015. "This is a franchise, remember, that gave us all-time pitching great Tom Seaver and Marvelous Marv Throneberry, who resides only in the Quip Hall of Fame."

Former Mets executive Al Harazin dreamed up the iconic apple as a way to further the team's 1980 marketing slogan, "The Magic is Back," according to the team's former vice presdient of business, Dave Howard. Similarly, a *New York Daily News* article from 2008 says former director of promotions Joe Donohue and his assistant, Jim Plummer, also deserve credit for the idea, which was inspired by the popular '80s trend calling New York City, "The Big Apple." "My feeling of the apple has really changed over the years," Dave Howard told ESPN.com after leaving the organization. "At first, I remember thinking, *Well, it does seem a little cheesy.* But the positive change in perception for me was when I started to see it through the eyes of my children and when I started working for the Mets and then, over thousands of games there, in the excited reaction of the fans."

In 2008, 97 percent of fans voting on my website, MetsBlog.com, said the apple was the most important thing from Shea Stadium that needed to make its way to Citi Field. Similarly, Mets third baseman and current captain David Wright has repeatedly said on record that Mets players view the apple as an "icon," and it's something first-time

A child poses for a picture on the Home Run Apple. Formerly in Shea Stadium, this apple is now located between lots F and G at Citi Field.
(AP Images)

visiting players are always eager to see. Wright is the first player to make the new apple rise in Citi Field. Against the San Diego Padres on April 13, 2009, the team's first home game that season, he hit a home run. "It's the Big Apple," Darryl Strawberry said during an interview with the *Daily News* in 2008. "I have a lot of fond memories of making that thing come up. That apple has always been special to me; it means you've done something good." Interestingly, perhaps being aware of Strawberry's admiration, Shea operators raised the Apple halfway after he hit a home run in Yankee pinstripes while facing the Mets during 1998.

I've heard Mets chief operating officer Jeff Wilpon was not interested in recreating Shea Stadium, wanting Citi Field to be its own, new experience instead. I'd like to think polls like the one on MetsBlog. com, and other fan efforts like Andrew Perlgut's and Lonnie Klein's SaveTheApple.com, helped preserve the original apple. However, I know for a fact that the Mets already planned to bring the old apple and display it inside Citi Field by the left-field bullpen gate because they said so on a private tour of the development site in early 2008. Nevertheless, it's nice to see fan passion and team decisions were always in sync. "The apple represents the fun of the Mets," Klein told the *Daily News* in 2008. "They are kind of the upstart kids, and the fans really take that attitude to heart. The apple is part of that."

It took only one year, but eventually the old apple was moved from the bullpen gate, where it was difficult to find, to its current, more prominent location outside Citi Field. In 2015 I took my daughters, who are three and five-years-old, to Citi Field for their first Mets game. It's been more than a year since we were there, and every time I come home from a game, they ask me if I saw the Apple—and they're not talking about the one in center field. They loved the one outside in the parking lot, in front of which they took pictures and marveled at its size. It's literally the only thing they care about. More importantly, it's helping keep them on track to be Mets fans.

See the Mets on the Road

Bucket Rank: 🗑 🗑 🗑 🗑

Shea Stadium was charming, and Citi Field is elaborate and pristine. But regardless of what the building has or looks like, I will forever love both homes because I'm most happy when surrounded by Mets fans, who, I believe, hold the perfect balance between respect for the game, an appreciation for hard work, and our love of the team. That said, it's a lot of fun to see the Mets on the road in enemy territory and experience how the organization and game are viewed through a different set of eyes.

Obviously, there is no better—or worse—place to see the Mets away from Citi Field than at Yankee Stadium. The organizations are rivals, but it pales in comparison to the battle that occurs between the two sets of fans. Believe me, I know. My wife is a New York Yankees fan. I didn't talk to her for several days after the Mets lost to her team in five games to drop the 2000 World Series. Nevertheless, as rough as it can be when your favorite team loses, seeing the Mets in that ballpark is an intense event every fan should experience.

Prior to 1997 the Mets and Yankees only played each other in exhibition games in New York, which they called "The Mayor's Trophy," before the season started. In 1988 my dad took me to the preseason game at Yankee Stadium, where—at 11 years old—I was booed and heckled relentlessly by the young Yankees fans in front, behind, and to the side of us. It was traumatizing at the time, but I love the memory today because it sums up the inter-city relationship. Basically, no one is immune.

Major League Baseball instituted interleague play in 1997. Later that year, on June 16, the Mets beat the Yankees 6–0 during the first ever regular-season battle between the two crosstown rivals. They would go on to play 112 more times, during which the Mets are 22–34 at both Yankee Stadiums.

The most intense of battles occurred in 2000, when—during July of the regular season—Mets catcher Mike Piazza was drilled in the helmet by a 98-mph fastball from Yankees pitcher Roger Clemens. Watching from the stands, I feared Piazza might have been killed, as he dropped to his back. He was flat and motionless on the ground with his eyes shut and unresponsive. Eventually, a groggy Piazza got up with the help of his coaching staff. And while the majority of Yankees fans in attendance cheered with respect for his awakening, the two rowdy men behind us instead applauded Clemens. "He's fine, now get back to beating these bums, Roger," the man yelled toward the field, spilling his beer a bit as he sat back down in his seat.

Piazza and Clemens faced off again later that year in the World Series, again at Yankee Stadium, resulting in one of the most bizarre moments in October history, when Clemens threw Piazza's splintered bat at him. Also in that series, Mets fans in attendance felt the brief moment when it seemed the Mets could win the series, but instead their closer, Armando Benitez, blew a save, and the Yankees eventually won in 12 innings.

Several years later, also at Yankee Stadium, Mets first baseman Carlos Delgado had nine RBIs (including a grand slam) during a loud, 15–6 win while setting the team record for most RBIs in a single game. Of course, the next year at the same location, Mets second baseman Luis Castillo made headlines and was laughed at for dropping a routine pop-up with two outs as the Yankees went on to a walk-off, 9–8 victory.

I would not suggest wearing a Mets shirt while sitting in the Yankee Stadium bleachers. Home to the notorious Bleacher Creatures, Yankees fans in this section are legendary for their loud, rambunctious, sometimes funny, sometimes vulgar behavior before, during, and after games. Sitting a few rows back at the old Yankee Stadium, I watched an angry group of Creatures literally rip a Red Sox shirt off a loud Boston fan and throw it on field. The Sox fan sat quiet and shirtless the rest of the game.

According to a 2015 article in the *New York Daily News*, the Bleacher Creatures were founded by Yankees fan Ali Ramirez, who rang a cowbell to inspire Yankee Stadium during the 1980s and '90s. Ramirez passed away in 1996, and a plaque was installed in the old and new bleachers to honor his fandom. I find their rules and regulations to be a little strict, such as being unable to talk on the phone, though I do appreciate their commitment toward never doing the wave.

The fact is, if you're a baseball fan, regardless of who you root for, going to Yankee Stadium is like going to a localized version of the Hall of Fame. Their Monument Park, which is typically open 45 minutes before every day game, should give chills to any out-of-town fan. And their museum, which actually has a presenting sponsor each season, tells of the franchise's (and game's) history through exhibits, memorabilia, and impressive artifacts. If you have a ticket to the game, the museum is free of charge and absolutely worth walking through before you find your seat.

If I learned anything during my first trip to Wrigley Field during September 2013, it's that Cubs fans are the opposite of Mets fans. Cubs fans appear to love being Cubs fans more than they love the Cubs. The results of the game were seemingly secondary to the experience of wearing a Cubs jersey, singing songs, and partying before and after each contest, regardless of whether the home team won or lost. Mets fans, on the other hand, tend to care most about the standings, and the afterparty only matters if they win. I prefer the latter. However, every baseball fan should experience the love and wonder around Wrigley at least once in their lifetime.

The Cubs may currently play in the National League Central, but they actually have a long history with the Mets with their first matchup having taken place in May 8, 1962. The two franchises have met 729 times, during which the Mets are 172–198 at Wrigley Field. However, if you were at Wrigley during 2014 and 2015, you caught seven straight Mets losses, but won there during the 2015 National League Championship Series.

In 1969 the Cubs blew a 10-game lead in the final two months of the season to the Mets, who surged past them for the National League pennant en route to their first world championship. In Wrigley that July, the Mets took two of three to start their climb and were helped out by a pivotal three-run home run by Al Weis. The two teams would square off 36 years later in the NLCS, which closed out with the Mets celebrating a trip to the World Series on the grass at Wrigley Field.

However, while the action on field has been historic, the action outside in Wrigleyville is often where the real fun occurs. Wrigley Field opened in 1914, after which the neighborhoods between the streets of Halsted, Racine, Irving Park, and Cornelia created the borders to a baseball community like no other in baseball.

The 40-square-foot area is full of restaurants and bars packed shoulder to shoulder with loud, passionate, funny, and serious Cubs fans. The Cubby Bear, Sluggers, the Sports Corner, Murphy's Bleachers, Exodus, Mullen's, and the Ivy on Clark are all classic destinations. Heaven on Seven and Tuscany on Clark have terrific Italian food. If you're looking to do some shopping, this is not the place to be—unless of course you're in the market for a Cubs, Bears, Bulls, or Blackhawks hat and jersey.

Also outside Wrigley Field, you'll find the Ballhawks hanging out on Waveland Avenue during batting practice and throughout the game waiting for a home run to sail over left field, out of the ballpark, and into the streets. Unfortunately, this has become more difficult because of Wrigley Field's expansion in 2015, but fans still gather, waiting, looking up in to the sky.

The Ballhawks became famous in 1989, when Cubs outfielder Andre "the Hawk" Dawson hit a home run onto Waveland that led to half a dozen fans fighting over the souvenir. The man that wound up with the baseball, Neal White, was later invited to discuss the melee on air with legendary broadcaster Harry Caray, after which hundreds of fans lined the street hoping for the same result.

"I think seeing a game at Wrigley Field is something any baseball fan should do. No matter your team fandom, the place is historic," Chicago resident and Mets fan Julie Bronder, owner/blogger at ChicagoMetsFan.com, told me. "As a Mets fan and going to games at Wrigley dressed in Mets apparel, I've always been welcomed without any hostility. Walking the main concourse is a treat that not many stadiums have anymore because of how old and tight it is. Taking the first steps up to the field level provides a view you'll always remember. By far, the most memorable Mets game I've seen at Wrigley was in 2015 when the Mets won the NLCS. It's a memory and experience I'll never forget."

Similar to the Bleacher Creatures at Yankee Stadium, Wrigley Field is home to the Bleacher Bums. "No one is off limits, and verbal abuse is just part of the experience," veteran sportswriter Paul Sullivan wrote in a 2015 column for the *Chicago Tribune*.

This is true. However, speaking as a Mets fan, I can say the Wrigley Field bleachers in left and center field are significantly more welcoming than those in the Bronx. There are also more nuances worth checking out in Chicago, such as "the well," a standing-room only, moat-like area that runs from the flagpole in left field above the legendary ivy and along the curve of the outfield wall.

Wrigley's bleachers are separated from the rest of the ballpark. They have their own private entrance, and other ticket holders cannot enter their section. Similarly, bleacher tickets do not allow you to enter the rest of the ballpark—only the bleachers. By doing this, it makes the experience feel like a private party and the place to be if you want to catch a game in the sun, drink beer, taunt and be taunted, and surround yourself with die-hard baseball fans.

Go to Spring Training

Bucket Rank: 🗑 🗑 🗑 🗑 🗑

Spring training baseball does not count in the standings, which is why it's such an innocent and relaxing experience for people who love the game. It's a time of year when skill—not winning and losing—is the focus. In Flushing, Queens, during late February it's typically cold and colorless. But in Port St. Lucie, Florida, home to the team's spring training complex at Tradition Field, it's sunny, typically around 65 degrees, calm, and everything's in bloom. The atmosphere, accountability, and actions are in sync.

The team's pitchers and catchers report to camp during the third week of February with position players filing in five days later. The group's first official, full-team workout is two days later with their first Grapefruit League game usually scheduled during the first week of March.

It may be all about the game when the baseball season begins. However, in my experience, when it comes to spring training, the team workouts are more unique and enjoyable experiences for the fans. The complex at Tradition Field, located at 525 NW Peacock Boulevard, includes seven practice fields, all of which can be accessed through the stadium parking lot. It was built and completed in 1988, prior to which the Mets held their spring training in St. Petersburg, Florida. Initially, they called it the Port St. Lucie Sports Complex with the main field named after local real estate developer Thomas J. White. In 2004, however, the team partnered with Tradition—the mixed-use community developed a few miles south—to rename the stadium Tradition Field.

During the week or two before Grapefruit League games begin, the team takes to a back field around 10:00 AM to stretch, after which they break off in to groups to work on drills, batting practice, and skills improvement. Fans are allowed to enter and roam the complex. It is not uncommon to see up to 100 Mets fans leaning on a fence, watching their favorite players take batting practice beneath the sun while chatting up a coach or front-office executive. It's casual, intimate, and allows for a view of the game—and the work involved—that is impossible to experience when the regular season begins.

Also, there are countless opportunities to interact with players, get autographs, and take once-in-a-lifetime photographs, especially after practice. There are fans who will stake out the exit to the players' parking lot, where some may stop their cars, roll down a window, and sign before leaving to head home. Immediately after practice, at least two or three high-profile players will stop, sign, and spend time with fans every day between practice field seven and the main stadium.

Tradition Field can hold up to 7,000 fans, many of whom set up for a picnic on the berm above the right-field fence. Unlike at Citi Field, the home dugout at Tradition Field is along the third-base side, as is the home bullpen. The ballpark opens one hour and 40 minutes before first pitch, during which players and coaches are usually accessible for autographs along the seats that separate fans from the field. When the Mets are playing at Tradition Field, the practice fields are open for fans to watch morning workouts, though they usually close around 30 minutes before the stadium opens the main gates to the ballpark.

The Mets play most of their Grapefruit League games against the Miami Marlins, Toronto Blue Jays, Washington Nationals, Houston Astros, Atlanta Braves, and St. Louis Cardinals with a one-off game against the New York Yankees, Boston Red Sox, and Detroit Tigers peppered in throughout March. The Marlins are the closest road team, playing roughly 40 minutes away at Roger Dean Stadium in Jupiter, Florida. The Blue Jays, who play nearly three and a half hours away at Florida Auto Exchange Stadium in Dunedin, Florida, are easily the farthest drive if you want to see an away game.

Port St. Lucie is on the east coast of Florida, the "Treasure Coast," as it's called. It is the eighth largest city in Florida, taking up 120 square miles with roughly 180,000 residents, according to the city's website. It's a two-hour drive south from Orlando but just 45 minutes north of West Palm, which is why most incoming fans land at Palm Beach International. It's a small, easy-to-navigate airport, repeatedly ranking among the least busy in America. Also, they have multiple Starbucks in case you need a jolt before your drive north.

By the way, I highly recommend budgeting time to cruise down Ocean Drive before your flight home. The sky high palm trees that line Royal Palm Way and the warm ocean breeze will create a peaceful end to your trip. St. Lucie West, the section of Port St. Lucie where Tradition Field is located, is a quiet, low-lying area spread out across 16 square miles, containing an endless supply of chain restaurant and stores.

Duffy's Sports Grill is the most popular sports bar and restaurant in the area. It's located less than a mile from the ballpark and packed full of Mets memorabilia and TVs with bar food, a bowling alley, an arcade, and a batting cage. It's a fun environment. Personally, I prefer Vine & Barley, the quaint wine and craft beer bar located a mile up the street. If Duffy's is where parents and kids go after the game, Vine & Barley is where they go when the kids are in bed.

There are several, popular brand-name hotels within a mile of Tradition Field, including extended-stay locations that have full kitchens, multiple rooms, and everything needed by a full family, or you can drive a few miles south and stay in Tradition, which is a quiet, pristine master-planned, mixed-use development. Tradition Square is anchored by a Publix supermarket and includes several shops, restaurants, parks, and fountains. In either case if you think you'll be visiting next spring, arrange for a hotel room sooner than later. Hotels tend to book up quickly through the winter, especially if the Mets played well the previous season.

By the way the Mets typically put their young players and coaches up at local hotels, which is fun, because you could end up staying in the same place. It's different every year, so you can't plan for it. But if you end up at the same location, which has happened to me before, you may end up doing laundry with a top prospect. In fact, I'm pretty sure I taught Wilmer Flores how to fold socks.

Visit the Bases from Shea

Bucket Rank:

In the middle row of Lot D in the parking lot of Citi Field, there is a marker shaped like home plate embedded in the pavement. This spot marks the exact location home plate rested in Shea Stadium. The pitcher's mound is 11 parking spaces northwest or roughly 500 feet from Citi Field. Second base is seven parking spaces behind the mound, first base stands two rows toward the Jackie Robinson Rotunda, and third base is roughly five rows across from that.

Shea Stadium was originally designed with two sets of motor-operated stands that allowed its field-level seats to rotate to make room for the New York Jets football team. However, after the Jets left for Giants Stadium in East Rutherford, New Jersey, in 1984, the Mets took over operation of Shea and retrofit it exclusively for baseball use. As part of the makeover, Shea Stadium was painted blue, and in 1988 90-foot tall neon signs of baseball player silhouettes were added to the building's exterior.

The Shea Stadium markers in the Citi Field parking lot each feature a separate engraving that resemble the classic neon designs. The embedded home-plate marker displays the catcher symbol, the pitcher's mound shows the neon pitcher, first base displays the neon hitter symbol, second base shows the neon base runner, and third base features the player catching a fly ball.

The markers create a fun, tangible reminder of Shea Stadium, which was officially knocked down February 18, 2009. The demolition, which began in October the previous year, might have started later had the 2008 season not ended the way that it did. The Mets had a three and a half game lead over the Philadelphia Phillies in the National League East on September 10 but lost 10 of their final 17 games and were eliminated from division contention with one game left in the season. The wild-card remained a possibility until—for the second consecutive year—the Florida Marlins ended New York's season in the final game, winning 4–2. The loss, coupled with a win by the Milwaukee Brewers earlier in the day, rewarded Milwaukee the National League's wild-card, making September 28, 2008, the final game ever played in Shea Stadium.

There will always be Mets fans who stand on this ground and only remember the brutal last game and the melancholy, bittersweet, farewell ceremony to the ballpark that followed on field. However, other Mets fans have found more positive ways to use the markers.

The Citi Field parking lots are available to be used for a variety of events with the Shea footprint serving as the field for wheelchair softball tournaments and countless Wiffle Ball and pick-up games. After news that former Mets catcher Gary Carter had passed away from brain cancer in 2012, fans used the home-plate marker as a memorial. Candles, Mets hats, flowers, equipment, baseball cards, and messages were left as a tribute to Carter, who was adored by fans and former players for his big smile and love for the game.

I often stop at the pitcher's mound to reconnect with personal memories and moments from growing up a Mets fan while going to games with my family and friends. I grew up expecting to pitch for the Mets in Shea Stadium. Obviously, that never happened. However, thanks to having a press credential with SNY, I did get to stand on the mound and fake a pitch before the building turned off its lights that final night.

Chapter 4

Things to Hear

Get Metsmerized

Bucket Rank: 🗑️ 🗑️ 🗑️

In 1985 when the Chicago Bears were 10–0 and being heralded as the best team in the NFL, they hit the recording studio to cut "The Super Bowl Shuffle." The rap song was released three months prior to their win in Super Bowl XX, peaking at No. 41 in February 1986 on the Billboard Hot 100 chart.

In April of 1986, Mets outfielder George Foster felt his heavily favored Mets could cash in with their own novelty track. So with a 1–0 record and 161 games yet to be played in the regular season, Foster and teammates Darryl Strawberry, Dwight Gooden, Lenny Dykstra, Rafael Santana, Rick Aguilera, Kevin Mitchell, Tim Teufel, and Howard Johnson recorded "Get Metsmerized." According to author Jeff Pearlman's *The Bad Guys Won*, two local record producers, Jeff Gordon and Aaron Stoner, told Foster that—if he could convince a few teammates to join in—they could make a lot of money doing a track similar to what the Bears did the year before.

Unfortunately, whereas "The Super Bowl Shuffle" was sanctioned by the Bears and sent all proceeds to charity, Foster never got his team's approval and only planned to pocket the profit. As a result, the organization's front office held up the project through most of the summer, instead commissioning their own song and video, "Let's Go Mets," which was prominently featured in their official VHS yearbook, *A Year to Remember* after winning the World Series.

"Get Metsmerized," which included an extended version on the B-side, eventually hit music store shelves in August of 1986, at which point Foster had already been released from the Mets. To date, the album has sold just under 200 copies, according to Billboard. "Picture Vanilla Ice on crack, MC Hammer with half a tongue, and Kurtis

GET METSMERIZED LYRICS

Here are a few of the more painful lyrics:

Howard Johnson: "My name is Hojo, I'm here to say our team is going all the way. With pitching, power, speed, and style, results guaranteed to make you smile."

Tim Tuefel: "I'm Tim Tuefel, let me begin by saying I was once a Twin. They made the move, it feels just right. I've been Metsmerized. I see the light."

Rick Aguilera: "When they want a batter filled with terror, they call on me, Rick Aguilera. Slider's hot, I'm on the mound with cool control, I mow 'em down."

Darryl Strawberry: "Power and speed, ya know we've got, we're the beasts of the East. When you're hot, you're hot. When Dwight is in the groove, there is no doubt, the next three words that you'll hear are, 'three strikes you're out.'"

Dwight Gooden: "Dwight's my name, what can I say, you know they call me, Doctor K. Change-up, fastball, slider, the curve, step to the plate if you've got the nerve."

Lenny Dykstra: "I love to run down long fly balls, I catch them all, ain't afraid of no wall. I bunt, I run, and then I dive, it's a wonder…I'm still alive."

Kevin Mitchell: "I'm Kevin Mitchell, season's rook, I'm studying all the moves. I'm ready to cook, I've got it together, I'm ready to play, I'm up in the bigs, and I'm hoping to stay."

Blow without one iota of rhythm," Pearlman writes of listening to the song. "Now put them all together and subtract any remaining shreds of harmony, flow, cadence, and talent…make sure the lyrics don't exceed a second-grade reading level."

Pearlman is dead-on with his review. In his defense Mitchell at least uses Sugarhill Gang-style cadence that is reminiscent of "Rapper's Delight," but the rest of his teammates are awkward at best. For instance, "Gooden delivers his lines like he's reading a ransom note from his captors, and Strawberry's rhyming is so far off the beat that it practically rips a hole in the space-time continuum," author Dan Epstein wrote for FoxSports.com in 2014.

Actually, I would love to know what was going through Teufel's mind as he recorded his verse. It was just three months earlier that he was living a quiet life in Minnesota. Then, boom, he's traded to New York. And after literally playing one game with the Mets, he's in a studio recording a rap album.

The song is painful. However, I love it because it speaks volumes about the 1986 team's confidence, cockiness, and total lack of shame—three qualities that helped the Mets be successful on field, as well as legendary party animals off of it. That said, as Epstein wrote, "no amount of titles could ever justify their collective ineptitude on the mic."

Learn Stengelese

Bucket Rank: 🗑 🗑 🗑 🗑

In 1962 at the age of 71, Casey Stengel was talked out of retirement and hired by the Mets to lead their expansion team's inaugural season. He had managed the New York Yankees from 1949 to 1960, winning seven world championships. The day he was announced as manager of the Mets, he said, "It's a great honor to be joining the Knickerbockers," who had not played in the area since the Civil War. "Most people my age are dead at the present time," he continued, thus officially introducing Mets fans to "Stengelese," the term used to describe his legendary mix of insight and double-talk.

"I been in this game a hundred years, but I see new ways to lose I never knew existed before," Casey said of his abysmal, but lovable, 1962 squad, who went 40–120 that season.

Nevertheless, the upbeat Stengel hyped his team as the "Amazin' Mets," a label that has stuck—and has been justified—from that point forward.

Every time Stengel talked, he was equal parts frustrated and happy, confused and poignant, serious and happy. He often contradicted himself, mangling phrases and inventing language. Yet, somehow, he made total sense. To Stengel, a doubleheader was "a double-headed game." If you were a rookie, you were either a "green pea," which meant you weren't good yet, or you were a member of the "youth of America," which meant you had potential. If you were "embalmed," you were in a slump. "Plumbers" were good infielders. If you were "fairly amazin'," you were a great player, but if you were a "road apple," it meant you were terrible.

Nearly one million Mets fans hit the Polo Grounds to see Casey's Mets in 1962. By comparison, 1.5 million fans went that season to Yankee Stadium for the franchise that had been in existence 61 years and already won 19 championships. When managing the Yankees in his prime, Casey was viewed as one of baseball's sharpest in-game tacticians. "I never saw a man who juggled his lineup so much and who played so many hunches so successfully," Hall of Fame player, manager, and team owner Connie Mack was quoted as saying in 1960.

Hall of Fame pitcher Warren Spahn played for Stengel when he managed the Boston Braves in 1942 and then joined the Mets in 1965. "I'm probably the only guy who worked for Stengel before and after he was a genius," Spahn said.

Stengel understood his role during his first season with the Mets. Hall of Fame baseball executive George Weiss hired Stengel to manage the Yankees. Then, when Weiss was hired to run the expansion Mets, who were clearly going to be a bad team, he convinced his old friend, Casey, to help make the game fun and entertaining.

According to a 1965 report by the *New York Daily News*, Stengel was believed to be earning $90,000 a season to lead the Mets. Based on inflation he would be the 13th highest paid manager by today's standards.

Stengel left the Mets in 1965 at 75 years old when he broke his hip and was forced to retire. His teams finished in last place all four years. However, Casey remains one of the most popular figures in franchise history. "Casey made the Mets," team owner Joan Payson said when he retired.

In the years after he left the Mets, Stengel spent his time speaking to local ballplayers graduating from high school and college, all of whom were considered possible draftees. He addressed them and their parents and encourage them to be part of the Mets. "Join the Mets, there is quick advancement," he would tell them with a wink and smile.

In 1969 Gil Hodges and the Mets won their first world championship. Al Jackson, Tug McGraw, Cleon Jones, Ron Swoboda, Kevin Collins, Bud Harrelson, and Ed Kranepool—each of whom was on the 1969 roster—all played for Casey during the organization's first four seasons.

BEST OF STENGELESE

Here are my 10 favorite Stengel quotes, which are the definition of Stengelese:

1) "Finding good players is easy. Getting them to play as a team is another story."

2) "Don't cut my throat. I may want to do that later."

3) "Good pitching will always stop good hitting and vice versa."

4) "He's a great hitter until I play him."

5) "You gotta lose 'em some of the time. When you do, lose 'em right."

6) "There comes a time in every man's life, and I've had plenty of them."

7) "He's the only defensive catcher in baseball who can't catch...I got one that can throw but can't catch, one that can catch but can't throw, and one who can hit but can't do either."

8) "Most ballgames are lost, not won."

9) "Without losers, where would the winners be?"

10) "The secret of successful managing is to keep the five guys who hate you away from the four guys who haven't made up their minds."

Listen to Bob Murphy

Bucket Rank: 🗑️ 🗑️ 🗑️ 🗑️ 🗑️

From 1962 to 2003, Bob Murphy was the "Voice of Summer in New York." He always was calm, joyful, grateful, and reliable, greeting us each night and day on the radio for Mets baseball. "Murphy was as much a part of Mets baseball as any of the players who have worn the blue and orange since 1962," Kevin Czerwinski wrote for MLB.com when Murphy passed away in 2004. "He was a friend on air, calling games in a simple, yet classic manner."

Murphy called his last game for the Mets on September 25, 2003. Earlier that night, the team honored him at Shea Stadium and announced that their radio booth would forever bear his name. "The Mets have provided me with a way of life," Murphy said that night. "Let me tell you fans how much I love you and how great you've been. Thanks for allowing us to be a part of your life. I've loved this so much and enjoyed this so much. I'd still be going strong if I felt as good as I did a few years ago."

Murphy, who called more than 6,000 Mets games, died less than a year later at a hospice in Palm Beach County, Florida, from lung cancer. He started every game upbeat with an appreciative tone and ended every win with "The Happy Recap." The origin of this phrase is unknown, he later said, though he believed he owed this level of positivity to Mets fans after every win. "I don't exactly remember how that came about or when I first used it," Murphy told reporters in 2002. "But a couple of the guys in the locker room told me it was real corny, so I stopped using it. And, boy, did the mail start pouring in asking, 'Where's my Happy Recap?' So, I put it back in and have been using it ever since."

Beloved announcer Bob Murphy acknowledges fans during his retirement ceremony in 2003. (AP Images)

His humble, everyman voice, plus his love of the game and appreciation for his craft—coupled with the crackle on AM radio— is something that can instantly warm my heart. Without hearing a word, I can shut my eyes and imagine his voice. Murphy is my backdrop to countless nights falling asleep as a kid on a school night, listening to his voice fade on my clock radio. Later in life, I remember driving home from Shea Stadium in the dark, using his timbre to stay awake on the Merritt Parkway as he recalled each moment from the game I just attended. "Hearing Murphy's voice during the first radio broadcasting during spring training was my official sign that winter was ending, and hope was alive again," Isaac from Teaneck, New Jersey, told me on Twitter.

Vin Scully's TV call for NBC is mostly associated with the ground ball through Bill Buckner's legs during Game 6 of the 1986 World Series. However, in my mind, I hear Murphy.

"And a ground ball trickling," he began, sounding depressed about the likely outcome. "It's a fair ball…gets by Buckner! Rounding third is Knight! The Mets will win the ballgame. The Mets win, they win!"

Scully called the play the way 24 fanbases were seeing it from home, which is exactly what he was supposed to do. Murphy, however, called it like Mets fans felt it. We were happy, and he was happy.

Murphy studied petroleum engineering and called sports at Tulsa University. In college he broadcast minor league hockey and baseball games, after which he began calling University of Oklahoma football games. He later developed a friendship with Curt Gowdy, with whom he called minor league baseball in Oklahoma. In 1954 Gowdy invited him to be his radio partner broadcasting Boston Red Sox games, which he did until 1959. He joined the expansion Mets in 1962, after calling two seasons with the Baltimore Orioles. "Bob had the most focus of any announcer I've ever known," Gary Thorne, Murphy's former partner and current announcer for MASN, told me in 2016. "He stayed completely in the game for the entire time and he was always a professional about it."

THE BEST OF BOB MURPHY

To know Bob Murphy, feel his passion, experience his enthusiasm and smile, do yourself a favor and listen to (or re-listen to) these five calls:

Mets Win the Pennant, September 24, 1969: "The crowd is chanting, 'We're No. 1!' The Mets made up 15-1/2 games since the 13th of August. Lou Brock is on second, and Vic Davalillo, the runner on first with one man out, ninth inning, 6–0 New York. Gentry pitching, working hard here against Joe Torre. Now in the set position, here's the pitch, ground ball hit to shortstop. Harrelson to Weis, there's one, first base, double play! The Mets win! It's all over! Oh, the roar going up from this crowd! An unbelievable scene on the field, as fans are pouring out on the field."

Lenny Dykstra's Home Run to Win Game 3 of the NLCS, October 11, 1986: "Dykstra, the man they call 'Nails' on the Mets ballclub is waiting. Now the pitch, and it's a high fly ball hit to right field. It's fairly deep, it's way back, by the wall...a home run! A home run! The Mets win!"

Game 6 of the World Series, October 25, 1986: "Mookie Wilson still hopes to win it for New York, 3–2 the count, and the pitch by Stanley. And a ground ball trickling, it's a fair ball. It gets by Buckner! Rounding third is Knight! The Mets will win the ballgame. They win! They win!"

Mets Win the 1986 World Series, October 27, 1986: "The pitch on the way...he struck him out! Struck him out! The Mets have won the World Series! The dream has come true. The Mets have won the World Series, coming from behind to win the seventh game."

Bobby Jones' One-Hitter that Sent the Mets to the NLCS, October 8, 2000: "Here's the pitch on the way to Bonds...Fly ball to center. Can he run it down? On the run, Payton...he makes the catch. It's all over! The Mets win it! Jay Payton makes the catch! A one-hit shutout, and they're all racing to the mound and mobbing Bobby Jones. What a magnificent game. The Mets have never had a better game pitched in their 39-year history than this game pitched by Bobby Jones."

Thorne also told me of some amazing moments he spent sitting at the bar after games during the 1980s, talking baseball with Murphy and Ralph Kiner, who was a Hall of Fame player and Mets TV broadcaster from 1962 until he died in 2014. "I mean, you had two professional people who came at the game from a different angle," Thorne explained. "So, when they sat down and started telling stories, it was the story of baseball. They were great friends, and it was wonderful to see—Bob, who knew every detail about everything, and Ralph, who played in that great era of baseball during World War II and after, and you heard all of it. They knew all the names from the beginning of the 1900s all the way to the current day. I loved sitting there; it was a great experience."

Meet the Mets

Bucket Rank:

Prior to a game outside at Citi Field—or years ago at Shea Stadium—with the sun setting and the game yet to begin, happily floating down from speakers and circling the ballpark, "Meet the Mets" can be heard welcoming fans to a night of Mets baseball. They say it's our fight song, though that seems like an inappropriate term since it makes everyone that hears it smile rather than become aggressive. In fact, it's so light-hearted, bouncy, and fun, my daughters have made it part of our bedtime song catalogue.

The music and lyrics were written in 1961 by Ruth Roberts and Bill Katz and originally recorded by Glenn Osser's orchestra before the franchise even played their first game. Team president George Weiss, director of promotions Julie Adler, and the J. Walter Thompson advertising agency selected it among 18 other options. "We found out later that the PR people for the Mets actually contacted Ruth and commissioned her to write the song, but she still entered it into the contest," Sandra Piller, Roberts' daughter-in-law, told ESPN.com in 2015. "So I guess both stories are true—she got commissioned to write the song, but she also entered the contest and won."

Roberts and Katz also recorded "I Love Mickey," a tribute to New York Yankees center fielder Mickey Mantle recorded in 1956. The 45 rpm recording of "Meet the Mets" was sold for $1 outside the Polo Grounds during the 1963 season. The listing of an original recording recently sold on eBay for $105. Roberts, who died in 2011, also wrote songs that were performed by the Beatles, Buddy Holly, and Dean Martin, though her most popular recoding will forever be "Meet the Mets." "It surprised her that the song lasted that long," her brother, San Roberts, told ESPN.com. "I think she thought it would last a year, maybe two."

In 2014 ESPN.com polled more than 11,000 voters, and they named "Meet the Mets" the best team song in Major League Baseball. Obviously, I agree. The original instrumental, which is beautiful in its simplicity, will forever make me think of waiting in line for tickets outside Shea Stadium. And the peppier, 1980s version produced by WFAN brings me back to secretly listening to broadcasts of games on the radio when I was supposed to be sound asleep.

In 1975 "Meet the Mets" was re-recorded by WOR in a late '70s, disco-style that I try to ignore. Similarly, for the 2009 season and the opening of Citi Field, WFAN instead cut to the instrumental version just before the singer says, "Hot dogs, green grass all out at Shea." Thankfully, that same season, the Mets began playing the original version—in its entirety—between innings at Citi Field. Of course, when it comes to playing "Meet the Mets" in stadium, nothing compares to Shea Stadium organist Jane Jarvis's rendition, which she played before every home game during her 16-year tenure with the team.

In 2015 after the Mets defeated the Los Angeles Dodgers in the National League Division Series, Rep. Adam Schiff (D-CA) made good on a bet with Rep. Steve Israel (D-NY) by singing "Meet the Mets" on the House floor. Thankfully, C-SPAN was there to broadcast it in all its glory.

The week after the Mets clinched a spot in the World Series, Billy Joel invited Steve Miller and John Mayer on stage at Madison Square Garden for their own rendition of the song. And six days later, Mr. Met conducted an orchestra and chorus in a performance of the song outside of the city's Metropolitan Opera. "Meet the Mets" has also been sung on *Seinfeld*, *Everybody Loves Raymond*, and by countless parents and children on YouTube.

Like any team song, despite changes in ownership, players, and uniforms, "Meet the Mets" is a catchy, upbeat, enduring link between the Polo Grounds and Citi Field. I might have grown up on Darryl Strawberry, you may forever admire Tom Seaver, you may have seen 1973, and I was there in 2006, but we all know the lyrics to "Meet the Mets."

· ·

Chant "Let's Go Mets!"

Bucket Rank:

There is a moment during every Mets game when there is no stadium music. Tension or potential defeat is in the air. The only recognizable sound is the quiet murmur of crowd noise, as everyone waits anxiously for the next pitch. And then out of nowhere in the silent distance, a hopeful, courageous, anonymous fan will scream, "Let's! Go! Mets!"

I love this person.

Their bellow isn't set to a predetermined rhythm. There's no definable cadence. It isn't prompted by the scoreboard or a traditional moment in the game. It's innocent, desperate, and authentic and captures everything that is great and torturous about being a fan.

I also love hearing this chant outside—before and after the game. There is a spot between the Mets/Willets Point train station and Citi Field where fans magically hit a wall of energy before the game. It's not visible, but it clearly exists because in this location you will almost always hear someone clapping or tapping the chant's three consecutive staccato beats. *Clap! Clap! Clap! Clap! Clap! Clap!*

However, the absolute best spot to hear "Let's Go Mets" is in the stairwells leaving the ballpark. Why? Because it means the Mets won a big game. In both Citi Field and Shea Stadium, the concrete walls that entombed them created a 40 to 50-foot tall echo chamber perfect for screaming fans after a win. The chant rises and falls in waves. We do it, they do it, the other stairwell does it, and so on, and so on, and before long it's just one, loud, massive mess of fun, swirling in and out of ears and making people smile.

In 1999 after the Mets beat the Atlanta Braves 4–3 in the 15th inning of Game 5 of the National League Championship Series, thousands of fans cheered "Let's Go Mets" from the time we left our seats, went down the exit ramps, walked through the parking lot, and got into our cars or seats on the train. In fact, when leaving the parking lot and driving with the windows down, I could still hear "Let's Go Mets" echoing from inside the stadium. Like the rain that night, the chanting never stopped.

Citi Field is less raucous than Shea Stadium. I assume this has something to do with the ticket prices, number of suites, and corporate sponsorships. That said, Citi Field is a more pleasant environment. As a father of two girls, if I had to choose one of the two buildings to take my family to see a game, I'd take them to Citi Field. However, if I'm going with my buddies, looking to have a few beers and yell at the opposing team's bullpen, I'd have rather been at Shea.

That is until the 2015 postseason, when Citi Field finally rocked. The Mets and Dodgers were tied 1–1 in their National League Division Series when Citi Field finally hosted their first ever postseason game on October 12, 2015. The crowd was anxious from the start. "Let's Go Mets" chants would start but quickly fade, especially when the Mets and Matt Harvey fell down 3–0 in the top of the second inning. Then, Curtis Granderson hit a bases-clearing double in the bottom of the second, the Mets took the lead, and Citi Field exploded. Later after a home run by Yoenis Cespedes essentially put the game away, leading the Mets to a new franchise record for runs scored in a postseason game. Mets fans totally lose their minds.

The usual, rhythmic "Let's Go Mets" was replaced by people yelling, "Let's Go," followed by a long "Mets" until their voice gave out. People were just screaming it, smiling in shock, waving orange home-run towels, jumping on seats, jumping off seats, high-fiving, hugging, and totally ignoring the fact that a game was still being played. It was wonderful and great to see.

It's wasn't just Mets fans that sang "Let's Go Mets" during the 2015 postseason. Chipper Jones may be their all-time greatest nemesis. He's a rival but is also a fan of our fans. He's never been a true enemy despite hitting .309 and 49 home runs against the Mets during his 19-year career. His Braves love him so much that they inducted him into their team Hall of Fame and retired his No. 10 during 2013. However, in October of 2015, as the Mets and Los Angeles Dodgers prepared to square off in the NLCS, Jones belted out a "Lets Go Mets" chant during an interview with WOR's *Mets On Deck* pregame show. "We are clearly living in the end of times," Braves fan Demetrius Bell wrote the next day for SBNation.com's Talking Chop.

There is a contingent of Mets fans that started adding a fourth beat to the chant during the early 1990s. In place of the silent beat between chants, people started filling the dead air with "Hoo." So instead of just "Let's Go Mets," it turned in to, "Let's Go Mets, Hoo." Personally, I don't like this. And I'm not alone. According to a Twitter poll I conducted, 79 percent of the more than 1,200 voters agreed. My friend, Brian Erni, is in the opposite camp. "My uncles did it, and I learned it from them," he told me, defending his choice. "It's what I grew up with. My dad and I are 'Hoo'ers.'"

In either case, whatever the form, "Let's Go Mets" is without question one of the most recognizable chants in sports, thanks in large part to a song recorded by the team and Shelly Palmer in 1986. In July of that year—with the Mets 27 games up on the St. Louis Cardinals in the National League East—advertising executives Jerry Della Femina, Bob Sherman, and John Olken commissioned Palmer to compose and produce an official theme song for the team. "So much of my job and focus was to build and maximize the brand of Mets baseball," Drew Sheinman, former Mets vice president of marketing, told *Rolling Stone*. "The biggest challenge was getting our management on board and getting Davey Johnson, a traditionalist baseball guy, to accept why we would even step outside the baselines to do something so entertainment-driven. Once they understood the long-term objective, everyone was very supportive."

The song, which reached gold, is good. It works. However, the music video, which reached triple platinum, is downright amazing. "You have to put yourself in the 1986 mind-set when VHS tapes were big," Palmer told *Rolling Stone*. "The ad agency came to me in July of 1986, and they had the most outlandish idea. They thought it'd be cool to have a Mets video and a half-hour making of documentary, too."

In the four-minute video, Palmer brilliantly captured the essence of New York in the 1980s and the city and team's enthusiasm and confidence about the Mets. The presentation is colorful, silly, and energetic, including a barrage of game highlights and an over-the-top collection of local servicemen and women; fans in half shirts; Mets hats and satin jackets; smiling players; and "celebrities," such as Twisted Sister, Howard Stern, Joe Piscopo, Dr. Joyce Brothers, and Cameo. "I'm a die-hard Yankee fan, but I'm a baseball fanatic, so when the Mets called, it was so exciting," Piscopo said in 2015 about his appearance in the video. "It's all about the greatness of New York."

It's so upbeat and ridiculously awesome that if I'm having a bad day, watching this video will instantly make me smile and ensure that I'm not taking life too seriously.

Chapter 5

Things to Read

Check out The Bad Guys Won

Bucket Rank: 🗑️ 🗑️ 🗑️ 🗑️

The 1986 Mets were a turning point for me as a baseball fan. At 10 years old, I left that season thinking baseball was what these guys had been known for, which was a loud, brash, bold style of baseball on the field and a louder, more brash, more bold lifestyle off of it.

And yet from that moment on, the 1986 Mets were systematically taken apart while the business of baseball took over. The game slowly became more corporate with every passing season. I used to think this was simply my perception as a maturing young man. However, thanks to award-winning former *Sports Illustrated* baseball writer Jeff Pearlman's 2004 book, *The Bad Guys Won! A Season of Brawling, Boozing, Bimbo Chasing, and Championship Baseball,* I confirmed that my 1986 heroes were simply *that* unique.

"It wasn't just guys destroying a plane. It was guys destroying a plane after an emotional roller coaster. There's a difference," Mets relief pitcher Randy Niemann told Pearlman about the infamous flight from Houston to New York after the 1986 National League Championship Series. I love this quote because it crystallizes my understanding and appreciation of that time, which is that no 25-man roster ever behaved off the field and succeeded on the field like these guys— before or after 1986. They weren't a turning point. They were an amazing, unique aberration, who, though no parent would endorse their behavior, were beloved for it.

Pearlman takes the reader inside the 1986 locker room, 162 regular season games, the postseason, World Series, the celebrations, and the player's personal lives. The group won games; invented curtain calls;

JEFF PEARLMAN Q&A

Matthew Cerrone: "How did you come to write a book about the 1986 Mets?"

Jeff Pearlman: "When I started to think about what really got me into baseball, what gave me that spark and enthusiasm, it was the 1986 Mets. I was a 14-year-old kid growing up in Mahopac, New York, and I loved that team. I loved it. I never really thought that there was a good book on the 1986 Mets that had been done. There were a couple of autobiographies back when the team won, but they were kind of rushed out. So I thought it would be a great book to do and story to tell because that cast of characters are exciting, and the baseball is awesome, and people remember that team so fondly."

MC: "Why did New York City go *so* wild for that team in 1986 in a way they never did about a single championship won by the 1990s Yankees?"

Jeff Pearlman: "There's certainly always been a passionate legion of Yankees fans, who love that tradition and pinstripes. However, it's hard to emotionally connect with and relate to guys like Derek Jeter, Jason Giambi, Hideki Matsui, Jorge Posada, etc. because they don't give you too much to go on. Most of their answers were cliched. You didn't see them hanging out in New York City. They're great baseball players, and people appreciate them for that, but I don't think New York City had the same emotional tie to those players like they did to the 1986 Mets, who were clearly a part of the city's fabric. There was more of an emotional tie to those Mets."

MC: "Also, I think the way Darryl Strawberry, Doc Gooden, Keith Hernandez, Gary Carter, Davey Johnson, and the rest of the team carried themselves—the way they played, won, and partied—was a reflection of New York City in the 1980s. I always felt the city embraced them more for that reason because they were proud of them in a way they couldn't be proud of Joe Torre's professional, buttoned-up Yankees."

Jeff Pearlman: "Absolutely. New York in 1986 was a very grimy place. I say it in the book, and it's really true. I mean, you could actually go to Times Square, buy cocaine, find a hooker, and snort it with her in the streets. There was graffiti everywhere. It was a dirty, grimy place, and the Mets were a dirty, grimy baseball team. In those days, you could go to a bar like Finn McCools on Long Island or Rusty Staub's and you'd see Lenny Dykstra and Bob Ojeda and Wally Backman and Strawberry and Gooden. These guys were accessible and they were so into being baseball players in New York. It was really a part of their soul. They oozed that. You'd go to Shea Stadium, and it would be pretty easy to get their autographs because they'd be out there signing. There was an accessibility and a cohesion with the city that I don't think a modern ballplayer probably in any city ever had [or has now] in the same way."

MC: "Unfortunately, what goes up, must come down. Do you think what made that team so great and so in sync with the city is also what made them fall apart and only win one championship?"

Jeff Pearlman: "I think we'll never know the answer to that. I think what really caused the demise of that team was then-GM Frank Cashen. He didn't like what was going on. He knew about the gambling and the drinking and he didn't really like what he heard. I think after that season, he and his assistant general managers decided that they needed to change the makeup of the team a little bit. The first guy they got rid of was Kevin Mitchell because they thought he was leading Gooden and Strawberry in a bad way. It was an erroneous belief, but one they followed through on. I think it's possible that substance abuse and excess would have brought that team down if it had been kept together for a number of years. But I think Cashen jumped the gun on disbanding them, so—sadly—we'll never know the real answer to that question.

Gary Carter culminates 1986 by jumping into the arms of Jesse Orosco after winning Game 7 of the World Series. Jeff Pearlman's book perfectly depicts that fascinating season. (AP Images)

trashed hotels, bars, and airplanes; were arrested; and left a trail of trophies and tragedy in their wake.

With chapters titled "Food Fight," "Metsmerized," "Drinking Days," "Revenge," and "Never Death," among 15 others, Pearlman's *The Bad Guys Won* immortalizes what I believe is the last great wild bunch of baseball players, all while he provides an undercurrent looking into what could have been—had the group not been disbanded the following season.

Prior to the book's publication, I did the following interview with Pearlman, during which we talk about several of its better stories, but these exchanges best capture the tone and temperament of the book.

. . . .

Learn About Alderson in Baseball Maverick

Bucket Rank: 🗑 🗑 🗑

In 2009 the Mets hit bottom. In addition to winning just 70 games and suffering a barrage of injuries, their principle owners grew further embroiled in the fallout from the largest financial scam in American history. The next season was barely better, after which general manager Omar Minaya was fired. At the suggestion of then-commissioner Bud Selig, the Mets replaced Minaya with Sandy Alderson.

In his outstanding book *Baseball Maverick*, author Steve Kettman profiles Alderson's impact on baseball and his work helping to stabilize the Mets. "My take on it, having talked with Selig, is that—whatever the exact state of knowledge was about how bad it was going to get for the Mets at that time in late 2010 when Alderson was hired—it was clear to Wilpon, Saul Katz, and Selig that there was not going to be a quick fix to getting the Mets to move forward," Kettman told me in 2015. "They knew it was going to take someone like Alderson, who had a steady hand and had earned enough respect that it would buy him some time to chart a course and follow it."

Kettman wrote that Alderson initially took the job with the Mets so he could spend more time with his father, John, who lived near the team's spring training complex in Port St. Lucie, Florida. Sadly, Alderson's dad, a former Marine infantry officer, died two weeks later after being struck by a car as he was crossing the street in St. Petersburg, Florida, according to the St. Petersburg police department. Alderson quickly returned to work, where ownership began cutting payroll in an effort to restructure debt, capital, and rebuild their franchise.

Kettmann is best known by baseball fans for helping Jose Canseco write his infamous memoir, *Juiced*. In *Baseball Maverick*, however, it is quite clear that Kettman is a huge fan of Alderson. Of course, so am I, which is probably why I enjoyed the book. And if you appreciate Alderson the same way, you'll enjoy it too.

The thing is—in addition to being an outstanding baseball executive—Alderson is also a former Marine with a dry wit. He's smart, self-aware, and has no need for bullshit. And while the book is full of stories about Alderson joining and rebuilding the Mets, it is also an inspiring story about service, hustle, and adaptability. It starts with Alderson's days as a Vietnam veteran, through his time at Harvard, after which he stumbled into a position with the Oakland A's during the early 1980s.

In time Alderson would rise from a consulting lawyer to a general manager who built a World Series winner with high-priced talent and enormous egos, including Canseco, Mark McGuire, Dave Stewart, and—one-time Met—Rickey Henderson. In the aftermath of the 1994 strike, Alderson's A's devolved into a small-market team in need of an edge that saved money but would keep them competitive on field. Alderson, who hired Billy Beane, helped spearhead an initiative to use statistical and evidence-based analysis as a way to identity inefficiencies in the market that Oakland could use to its advantage. Michael Lewis later coined this approach, "Moneyball," which was the title of his 2003 book that made Beane a baseball rock star and the subject of a feature film of the same title starring Brad Pitt in 2011. However, during the late '90s, "Beane was a baby duck following the big duck," Kettmann wrote.

Mets general manager Sandy Alderson, who announces a contract extension for manager Terry Collins in 2015, is profiled in the great read, Baseball Maverick. (AP Images)

According to Kettman, Beane essentially gave him the title of his *Baseball Maverick* book after the two spent an entire afternoon together in Oakland. "Alderson, for Beane, was this fascinating, dynamic character, who thought for himself, who knew what he knew, and was always looking for new ways to do things," Kettmann told me, when I talked to him about the book in early 2015.

In the span of 320 pages, we learn all sorts of interesting tidbits about the Mets. For instance, Alderson said he was close to firing Terry Collins in 2014, he should have asked more questions about the impact of Madoff's Ponzi scheme, and Jose Reyes rejected his $100 million offer before signing with the Miami Marlins. Alderson also discusses how he created public pressure on the San Francisco Giants to trade for Carlos Beltran, collected incoming cables from U.S. embassies while working for the CIA, pursued Robinson Cano, and talked to the Baltimore Orioles about R.A. Dickey, who he eventually sent to the Toronto Blue Jays for Travis d'Arnaud and Noah Syndergaard.

Kettmann's book, which was published April 7, 2015, was subtitled: *How Sandy Alderson Revolutionized Baseball and Revived the Mets.* The title was mocked relentlessly because at that point the Mets were just 305–344 during Alderson's time in Queens. Kettman discussed the criticism. "That's been fun," Kettmann told me. "You work four years on a book and it comes out. You're just hoping people know you are there—even if people are ripping you." Kettmann said "Maverick" traditionally means a person who thinks for himself and who was smart and shrewd. "'Baseball Maverick' doesn't mean, 'Great Baseball Guy,'" Kettman explained. "It means someone who upends the conventional wisdom. And in regards to Alderson, there's just no argument that this is what he did in baseball."

Apparently, Kettmann was right. In 2015, five months after the book was published, the Mets shocked baseball by winning the National League East and advancing to the World Series. Twelve months later Alderson would become the first general manager in 16 years to get the Mets to the postseason in back-to-back seasons. In other words the Mets were "revitalized."

. . . .

Click on MetsBlog.com

Bucket Rank: 🪣 🪣 🪣 🪣 🪣 (Author's Note: Obviously)

Obviously, I'm biased, since the reason I'm writing this book is because of my job writing MetsBlog.com. However, I feel I do the best work of any team sports blog online, and that's been true since I started in 2004. I believe this because, while other fans may be more individually passionate, more loyal, more knowledgeable, creative, or experienced, no fanbase is better at all of these things than Mets fans.

We are a five-tool fanbase. And because of that, I've been able to write 25 million words with 100,000 blog posts to tens of thousands of readers during the last 12 years. There is no other fanbase in sports that has this level appetite for information about a single subject.

In 2003 while taking a digital media class at the University of Maryland, I created a blog about the Mets. The objective was to pick a new medium and subject we were passionate about. I am a political junkie, and blogs were rising in popularity, mostly due to coverage of the Iraq War. It was a few years earlier that I discovered Bryan Hoch's MetsOnline.net, which was the first popular, online destination for Mets fans. The site was eventually shut down when team owners banded together to create MLB Advanced Media, the interactive media branch of MLB.

Hoch eventually landed at NJ.com where he wrote Always Amazin, a traditional-style blog about the Mets. It was this site that inspired me to pick the Mets for my digital media project. At the time I started,

FORBES.COM INTERVIEW

In 2012 I did the following interview with Forbes.com's Tom Watson, during which we discussed the ins and outs of blogging and what's great about the Mets online contingent.

Tom Watson: "It seems to me the Mets have the best network of blogs and semi-pro journalists in Major League Baseball. There's an incredible range of both opinion and analysis out there and some really strong voices. Why do you think that is—what about the Mets seems to attract writers and self-starters?"

Matthew Cerrone: "I'd like to take some credit for this since MetsBlog started in 2003 and I've hustled and worked very hard to keep innovating and changing what the blog is and what it means to online content. I think I've helped show what is possible and I believe that has inspired a lot of Mets fans to want to do the same. That said, it's New York City. There is no shortage of media and opinion. Also, Mets fans live for tomorrow. We're very much in the business of 'hope' and 'what's next,' talking trades, roster management, etc., all of which lends itself to information and blogging. I find most Yankees fans simply watch the game and take for granted that the team will be playing in October, so there is less day-to-day anxiety, making for less of a need to seek out day-to-day information. This is *not* the case for Mets fans, believe me."

Tom Watson: "You're a Mets fan, but you're also an entrepreneur working on a business that's closely related to your long-time avocation. How do you separate your status as a 'fan' with the guy running a growing enterprise?"

MC: "Being a fan is what makes the blog possible, so I don't separate it. I make a concerted effort to limit my access to what goes on behind the scenes, to help protect that innocence because being emotional and caring about baseball is a) something I don't even want to lose, and b) it fuels my passion for the blog, and that passion is part of what helps it connect with fans. Also from a business point of view, being a fan and talking with other fans is important because it lets me better understand the experience and people I'm trying to educate, inform, and entertain all day. I have an audience. I know they disagree and feel that is counter to what it means to be a reporter, and that may have been true, but times [and sports journalism] are changing and they'd be smart to change with it."

I was taking classes in journalism at Maryland, while working from home for the brilliant, legendary media relations pioneer Gary Stromberg.

Hoch would go on to cover the Mets for MLB.com, where he's still working, though he now covers the New York Yankees. He's the Godfather of Mets blogging, which is why the following quote is so meaningful to me. "I'm a big fan of what Matthew Cerrone has done with MetsBlog.com, having seen him launch it and grow it into something great," Hoch said in an interview with MetsMerized in 2010. "I know he's just as serious and devoted to what he's doing as I once was. It's fantastic that he has latched on with SNY, and that the Mets organization is now so receptive and aware of the influence blogs and the Internet carry among the fanbase. He really has become a must-read for fans of baseball."

My first thousand readers will remember the site without a custom domain name, with nothing but black text, and no comments, images, or sidebars on a generic Yahoo! Geocities page with a gray background. I simply logged my thoughts and opinions about each game, talked about trades, and what I wanted the Mets to do to be better. I was an out-of-market fan, and this was the best way I could stay connected to the team. And thankfully, other people spending their time online found it interesting and useful enough to keep reading.

The site was eventually named "MetsBlog," and I bought the corresponding domain name to go with it. I flirted with "MetsWeblog" because that is what the Internet was still calling them back then. But MetsBlog had a better ring to it, so I went with it. In hindsight that may have been the greatest decision of my life. The second best decision was adapting to a changing media landscape. I've always believed it's better to be a kingmaker than a king. So inspired by Hoch in 2005, as well as political bloggers Andrew Sullivan and Glenn Reynolds, MetsBlog shifted from a strict opinion site to one of aggregated news content and interviews enhanced by my own reporting and fan-perspective insights and analysis.

In an equally bold move, I stopped hiding behind an anonymous handle, put my name on the top of the site and my face in front of every opinion. I took ownership of my words but also offered myself up as a fellow fan, a tastemaker for readers to see as a friend, not just a resource.

In early 2006 I was offered an opportunity to do public relations work for a gubernatorial campaign in Connecticut, which was tempting since I had just gotten married and needed a more lucrative salary. However, it would have meant taking a hiatus from MetsBlog, which was being read by a few thousand people a day and finally earning money. Thankfully, friends and family—and my wife—encouraged me to stick with MetsBlog, which was clearly developing into a once-in-a-lifetime opportunity.

At that point MetsBlog was racking up a million page views per month. So late in 2006, I approached the team's recently launched regional cable network, SNY. I had online readers but lacked access; SNY had the opposite issue. It took a year, but we eventually formed a partnership. In time SNY would purchase MetsBlog and hire me to be their director of strategy for all digital content while continuing to be the lead voice on MetsBlog.

Today there are 10 to 15 blogs about the Mets that are run by fans, including MetsBlog. In 2005 there were 116. The quality is outstanding with the elite sites operating inside a specific niche that makes them unique and valuable in a noncompetitive way. MetsBlog has always been the best at summarizing existing stories comprised of all media while providing short, quick context from a fan's perspective. However, AmazinAvenue.com is the best option for statistical- and evidence-based analysis. MetsMerizedOnline.com is the best place to get a 360-degree view of multiple opinions. There is no one I would rather hear from on historical days in team history than FaithAndFearInFlushing.com. And MetsPolice.com is literally the only one of the bunch obsessed with what the Mets wear, say, and sell to their fans. There is something for everyone, which is necessary to satisfy our five-tool fanbase.

. . . .

Learn the Game from Keith Hernandez's Pure Baseball

Bucket Rank: 🗑 🗑 🗑 🗑

If you want to learn about baseball and specifically pitching from the perspective of the batter, there is no book better than *Pure Baseball*, which was written by former Mets first baseman, current SNY broadcaster, and baseball legend Keith Hernandez. No other player played the game with more fervor, passion, and intelligence than Keith Hernandez," Tim McCarver said. "I loved to watch him play."

In 272 pages the brilliant Hernandez provides a pitch-by-pitch analysis of every nuance during two games from June of 1993 (Philadelphia Phillies vs. the Atlanta Braves and the Detroit Tigers vs. the New York Yankees). He literally narrates every pitch, every sequence, as well as the most ordinary moments. As a result, he transports you into the mind of the pitchers, hitters, fielders, base runners, and managers.

In the Phillies-Braves game, he takes particular interest in a moment with Jeff Blauser on second base and Terry Pendleton coming to the plate for Atlanta. Pendleton had struggled to start the season but entered the game with an 11-game hitting streak. Hernandez briefly discusses Pendleton's poor splits against Phillies starter Danny Jackson, which creates a springboard for Hernandez to launch into the type of riffing that gives color to *Pure Baseball*. "Some managers place great stock in these mano-a-mano statistics, but I'm dubious, especially when the stat is a negative for the hitter. We're talking here about a total of 35 at-bats," Hernandez explains in the text, which drips with his sardonic wit. "Maybe Terry came up against Danny a couple of times when Terry wasn't swinging the bat well, or Jackson was throwing great or both. Or maybe Terry has just been hit with bad luck against Jackson. I got quite a few key hits off Nolan Ryan and a bunch of walks, so I was shocked to learn that I had something like a .170 batting average against him. I battled Nolan. I always felt I was a tough out for him, but you wouldn't know it from that batting average. Therefore, if I were looking down the bench for a pinch-hitter to use against Danny Jackson in some future game, I wouldn't hesitate to go with Terry Pendleton and I'm sure Bobby Cox wouldn't either."

In between moments like the above, he gets down to tactics and situations, such as base stealing, defensive alignment, bunting, productive outs, and the hit-and-run. But Hernandez's true brilliance shines when giving the reader an inside look at what is going on in the mind of the pitcher and batter. He walks through literally every pitch of both games. It is a lot to take in mentally, but his insights are unique and brilliant as he meticulously takes us through each moment's cat-and-mouse dynamic in a way that helps create a new understanding and level of respect for the game within the game within the game.

To those of us who watch Hernandez nightly on SNY, his quips and pet peeves are second nature. At this point we probably know them better than he does. But in *Pure Baseball* they're preserved forever in text. And—because I can't help but hear his voice in my brain while reading the book—his complaints turn from serious insight to comedic and insightful genius.

I can't get enough of his moaning about intentional walks, early-inning sacrifices, gaps in the outfield, pitchers who "nibble," and, of course, "fundies." I also can listen and read forever about how he breaks down the eternal, fundamental battle for control of the inside part of the plate.

Interestingly, while Tom Seaver goes in depth about *how* to throw in his *The Art of Pitching*, Hernandez actually gives more useful information because he takes you through the purpose of each pitch. Instead of talking only about mechanics and rotation, Hernandez supplies a needed context for multiple situations, when and why to use one pitch over another. As a fan situational knowledge and context are everything because it's all I have left to experience. For instance, when discussing how Phillies left-handed pitcher Danny Jackson used his "tailing fastball," Hernandez goes in depth on how right-handed and left-handed hitters were approaching him, not only dependent on the side of the plate they were standing, but also in the context of the situation, who was on base, what was the score, what was the count, and how fielders were set up behind him.

Hernandez then uses this opportunity to explain how—when facing someone who throws a more straightaway fastball—the hitter's approach will change. He then transitions to explaining the difference between a back-up and backdoor slider. "The right-handed pitcher facing the right-handed batter wants to throw the breaking ball on the outside corner. Why? If any breaking ball misses the target, it's usually to the left, outside, as the right-handed pitcher sees the plate," Hernandez explained. "Locating the breaking ball inside in this righty-righty matchup is even tougher psychologically because the pitcher has to aim almost behind the batter. So the tendency is even more to miss to the left. And if you aim at the inside corner but miss to the left, where does that leave the pitch? Over the inner half—the heart of the plate."

If you're wanting to not just learn the game, but understand why and how things happen the way they do, Hernandez's *Pure Baseball* is the only book you'll ever need.

Pick Up a Copy of The Worst Team Money Could Buy

Bucket Rank: 🗑️ 🗑️ 🗑️

The 1986 Mets were my first, full-season introduction to baseball. I loved that team. So when they were systematically broken apart during the next five seasons and the 1992 team was assembled, I had mixed feelings. I was no longer allowed to root for Darryl Strawberry, Lenny Dykstra, Keith Hernandez, and Gary Carter. However, to the tune of $44 million (or $250 million in 2015 dollars), Mets fans were given Eddie Murray, Bobby Bonilla, Brett Saberhagen, and Vince Coleman, all of whom were All-Stars at the peak of their careers. Things were looking up.

Unfortunately, despite having an unprecedented 13 millionaires on the roster, the 1992 Mets won just 72 games. And so *The Worst Team Money Could Buy* by veteran reporters John Harper and Bob Klapisch ended up becoming a yearbook for that terrible team and season.

Klapisch, who worked for the *New York Daily News* in 1992, and Harper, who was working for the *New York Post*, initially set out to write a book about the life of a sportswriter. "This is an era before the Internet, before ESPN, and people really had no idea what it was like to be a sportswriter, more specifically what it was like to be a baseball writer and what it was like in the clubhouse, what the players are like, and what they talked about and how they acted," Klapisch told me during a 2016 interview. "There was a life behind the curtain that only we, as sportswriters, had access to. And people loved to hear the stories...Doctors, businessmen, lawyers, they'd say, 'I wish I could be in your shoes, I love your job and love that you can go behind the scenes and experience baseball after the game.' So, Harper came to me and said, 'Let's write about it. We've told these stories, let's put them in print...We carved up a book proposal, went to Random House, and said, 'Ya know what, this is a pretty darn good team.' We figured we could use this championship team as the backdrop to life as a baseball writer in the early 1990s."

However, when it became clear that the Mets would not be winning a championship and instead end up among the worst rosters in franchise history, Harper and Klapisch switched gears and made their book less about journalism and more about the team's failure. "It was the wrong mix of guys; it was bad chemistry," Klapisch explained. "They had a weak manager in Jeff Torborg, who was afraid of the most powerful guys on the team. He lost control, they all hated the media, and they had nothing in common with the fans, who were still in love with the 1986 club. This was an entirely different era that had begun, and nobody was happy. Everyone was miserable."

The 1986 Mets are often portrayed as wild, crazy, and fun, living life to its fullest in a raw New York City, which celebrated the team's success on field. By contrast, Klapisch and Harper show us a different version of New York baseball players, capturing the 1992 team's arrogance, ego, anger, and paranoia. The authors also paint the organization's front office and ownership as meddling, misguided, and obsessed with dismantling their raucous and less-than-family-friendly championship team from six years earlier.

The Worst Team Money Could Buy is not a book that glamorizes baseball. In the span of 285 pages, you'll repeatedly read about "money-inflated egos," "spoiled ballplayers," "pampered, excuse-making millionaires," and "prima donnas." It is actually painful and awkward at times, especially since its set in the wake of a fleeting era most Mets fans hold dear in their hearts, but this is what I like about it. It's raw and honest and about a transitional time when MLB and its players were no longer being shy about being a business.

True to the book's initial intent, Klapisch and Harper also detail their role as sports reporters and storytellers. The duo are unusually honest about how they (and their industry) work to shape a team's narrative, which was not only based on the team's results, but also the characters in the clubhouse and how they related to the media.

In the end Klapisch and Harper produced an amazing diary of the 1992 season in Queens, which further detailed why the Mets had become so bad and out of touch with their fans between 1986 and 1992 all while also explaining life as sportswriters.

• •

Relive The Year the Mets Lost Last Place

Bucket Rank: 🗑 🗑 🗑

My first time regularly watching Mets baseball on TV was late summer of 1983, during which a 38-year-old Tom Seaver won nine games in his return season to the Mets. I was a seven-year-old that season, so Tom Terrific's place in franchise history was totally wasted on me. It wasn't until several years later, when I was 13 years old and reading *The Year The Mets Lost Last Place*, which was first published in 1969, that all those cheers and tears for Seaver in 1983 made sense.

The book, which is an easy-to-read 223 pages, is a fun, quick, real time snapshot that mostly focuses on nine crucial days in early July, when the Mets played the Chicago Cubs six times (three games each at Shea Stadium and Wrigley Field). The real drama occurs in the first two games, when the Mets got a dramatic, walk-off win that brought Jerry Koosman's wife to tears, after which Seaver nearly threw the franchise's first no-hitter.

Interestingly, the book's authors, Paul Zimmerman and legendary journalist Dick Schaap, chronicle 1969 in a fast-paced, minute-by-minute style that is befitting of modern day sports reporting, including using a dry, sarcastic humor that would make today's Twitter users proud.

The duo also include funny commentary and priceless stories about the past and present on-and-off-the-field lives of Seaver, as well as teammates Jerry Koosman, Tommie Agee, Jerry Grote, Ed Kranepool, Donn Clendenon, Art Shamsky, Ron Swoboda, Cleon Jones, Ed Charles, and others, all of whom captured the imagination of baseball. Conversely, the Cubs are treated as the enemy, "the bad guys," so to speak, which is something that rarely ever happens in baseball literature. Obviously, as a Mets fan, I like this approach.

The Mets had finished last, or second to last, in each of their first seven seasons. By the end of May at 21–23, it seemed like 1969 would be more of the same and likely end with the Mets being the laughingstock of baseball. Instead, they went an astounding 79–39 through the rest of the season, all on the backs of mostly ordinary players having career years. But the Chicago Cubs totally fell apart in September, as the Mets kept winning. In the end New York got a championship, and the Miracle Mets were born.

The thing I love most about this book is that it occurs during a time when the business of baseball is barely a consideration, let alone the focus as it often is now. Seaver, Koosman, and company are one of the last "teams" from a totally different era, the likes of which we will never get to experience in professional sports again.

In addition, despite taking place during the tumultuous year in American history of 1969, there is no reference to anything political, about Vietnam, or anything happening outside the world of baseball. It's a short, tight, detailed book on baseball…just baseball. As such, unknowingly, Zimmerman and Schaap put a romantic spin this era, creating a beautifully written, sustainable, lovable baseball story.

Chapter 6

Things to See

Log On to #MetsTwitter

Bucket Rank: 🗑 🗑 🗑

Mets fans need to complain and vent their paranoia, and Twitter provides the perfect, real-time home for people looking to let out those momentary thoughts, even if happiness is around the corner. #MetsTwitter is made up of thousands of die-hard Mets fans—young and old, male and female, optimistic and skeptical—all of whom regularly use the social network to talk about the team all day, all night, and all year.

According to the social media analytics company Klear, Mets fans typically make an average of 610,000 posts on Twitter, Facebook, and Instagram during a given month, the most in MLB. In the same time span, Yankees fans make 535,000 posts to the same social media sites.

Social Media Examiner and Shareable Data reported Mets fans made 475,500 tweets during the week the Mets clinched a spot in the 2015 World Series, which was the most in all of professional sports.

The interaction and outbursts on Twitter have no choice but to be brief because the popular social network only allows a message to contain 140 characters. The result is a beautiful and entertaining mix of unique interactions, intense emotions, optimism and skepticism, peace and support, irrational behavior, and a lot of opinions.

It's important to understand that these expressions exist for just that point of time. It's a digital stream of consciousness, creating a snapshot of that moment's reality—not the next one. In many cases, the Mets fan on Twitter who is voicing a negative opinion one minute is likely to be celebrating a contradictory moment a few minutes later. And this happens all game and for every news story.

Yoenis Cespedes played a major factor in getting the Mets to the World Series in 2015. In January the next year, multiple reports indicated he was close to signing a free-agent contract with the Washington Nationals, New York's biggest rival at the time. #MetsTwitter lost its collective mind. The depth and velocity of their panic was like nothing I had ever seen from it before. Minute after minute for a full day, it was nothing but a rainstorm of tweets firing jabs at the team's owners, screaming at the general manger, and giving up hope for 2016.

Cespedes signed with the Mets less than 24 hours later. And in an instant, all was right in the world of #MetsTwitter. Suddenly, ownership, and the GM were brilliant; Cespedes was again a god; and everyone was content with the roster and making plans for the World Series. "Sports bring out people's inner lunatic in a way that other industries only wish they could," Nathan Gismot wrote in 2015 for SBNation.com. "Twitter, for its part, is practically tailor-made for the proliferation of this gleeful madness."

This sense of belonging and community is one of many reasons why social networks are successful. "It's almost like we are having a nightly board meeting to discuss the state of our team," Greg Price, Mets fan and creator of FaithAndFearInFlushing.com told *Newsday* in 2015. "Mets fans are always looking for some sort of outlet, and I think we've wound up where we wound up—which is short, 140-character bursts and just this desire to be heard."

The @Mets official team Twitter account is often just as erratic, yet fun and useful, as any one of its 713,000 followers and fans. In a given day, @Mets may post content that is informative and useful but then later write something that is corny and poorly timed.

Nevertheless, they always do a terrific job marketing their players in this environment, helping to give fans a personality to rally around.

The @Mets and #MetsTwitter communities are very much responsible for initially branding Matt Harvey as the Dark Knight: here to save the Mets from their enemies. They encourage Noah Syndergaard to present himself as Thor, the mythological hammer-wielding Norse god. David Wright is Captain America, and Bartolo Colon was #BigSexy.

Syndergaard, in particular, has embraced using Twitter himself. In addition to being an intense and dominant pitcher, he is also a self-aware, funny, and confident 24-year-old guy. His tweets are perfectly timed and often pretty amusing. Within minutes of news that Bartolo Colon had left the Mets to sign a contract with the Atlanta Braves, Syndergaard posted a GIF of Will Ferrell from the movie *Anchorman*, in which he's screaming and crying in a phone booth. In July of 2015, when the Empire State Building was struck by lightning, he posted a photo of the moment and wrote, "Wasn't me," a reference to the thunder and lightning power of his alter-ego, Thor.

The Mets also use their Twitter account to connect with their fans. The account often answers questions and regularly conducts question and answer sessions with current and former players. In addition, @Mets is known to post recipes, raffles, and fund-raising opportunities for people in need. "Companies looking to reinforce brand loyalty and to reach new fans can look to the Mets for inspiration," said Solomon McCown & Company, a public relations firm in Boston specializing in business and public policy. "Social media has the ability to change or reinforce outside perceptions of an organization; in this case the humor presented through the Mets' Twitter posts reflects the team's change from a dour, hopeless club into one that projects joy and ambition at every turn."

#MetsTwitter is not the only hashtag used by Mets fans on Twitter. #TRAID is often used to describe a trade between the Mets and another team—proposed by a desperate and emotional fan—that has zero chance of ever happening. #BackToYouGare is a hat tip to former Mets sideline reporter and current FOX Sports broadcaster Kevin Burkhardt, who used to end all of his sideline reports by saying,

"Back to you, Gare" before tossing the segment back to his colleague and TV play-by-play announcer Gary Cohen. My favorite hashtag is #BlameBeltran, which was created by my friend and *USA TODAY* sportswriter Ted Berg to blame Carlos Beltran for any bad thing that happens to the Mets because that's what some fans used to do whenever Beltran did anything on field.

The team's beat reporters also get into the action, though they'd probably deny being part of #MetsTwitter. In some ways, they have their own community, goofing on one another during games despite sitting a few feet apart in the press box. They tweet game action, answer fan questions, reveal news and rumors, and take a ton of abuse. In some cases the abuse is understandable because there are reporters that stoke the fanbase's negative emotions. However, it's all in good fun, and everyone typically moves on from the moment.

The hyper-aware, detail-oriented, over-reactionary nature of Twitter has made some athletes, including some on the Mets, guarded for fear that their personality or behaviors will be ripped apart by fans and media. In 2014 former Mets pitcher Ron Darling told me that had social media existed in 1986, when his Mets won the World Series and were known for their wild off-field lifestyles, he and his teammates would have needed to be far more discreet. "I don't think we would have been around the city as much, which probably would have hurt how connected people felt to our team," he said. "I think today's players need to be very careful, but they also have a chance to brand themselves in ways we didn't."

In the end #MetsTwitter is essentially an online sports bar where fans can debate, celebrate, and commiserate. It's the same conversation that happens in barber shops, offices, living rooms, and any place fans gather to talk about their favorite baseball teams. "Engaging in the community of #MetsTwitter is unlike anything I've ever experienced," Megan Johnson wrote on her Boston College blog in 2013. "I can check #MetsTwitter at any point to find out an incredibly detailed play-by-play or I can just check it to find hilarious jokes about our beloved team."

#MetsTwitter is open to everyone, as long as you have a Twitter account. It doesn't matter if you're young or old, male or female, or the most positive or negative fan. And, just like real life, it includes nice people, rude people, funny people, and depressing people. It has led to legit friendships that now exist offline. It has brought people together that have created charitable causes, community events, and businesses. It's a wild place, but it's our place, and everyone is invited to join.

• •

Watch Kiner's Korner

Bucket Rank: 🗑 🗑 🗑 🗑

In 1963 Hall of Fame outfielder and Mets TV broadcaster Ralph Kiner began hosting what is considered the first ever postgame show, *Kiner's Korner*, which aired after every Mets home game on Channel 9. The concept was to have Kiner interview a celebrity at the stadium or player from that day's winning team, be it the Mets or their opponent, while showing game highlights and scores from around the league. It is now commonplace to see this on television now. But in 1963, though other networks had postgame shows, Kiner's was the first to include one-on-one interviews with people from the game.

Kiner began his playing career with the Pittsburgh Pirates in 1946, where aging Hall of Fame outfielder and legendary home-run hitter Hank Greenberg took Kiner under his wing. Kiner was an instant success and quickly considered one of most dangerous, right-handed home-run hitters in baseball, hitting more than 300 during his first eight seasons. He became known around baseball for beating up the left-field corner at Pittsburgh's Forbes Field, which fans eventually referred to as "Kiner's Corner."

The Mets honor former outfielder and broadcaster Ralph Kiner before Opening Day in 2014.
(USA TODAY Sports Images)

During his time playing for the Pirates, Kiner became friends with legendary singer and actor Bing Crosby, who was a part owner of the club. It was through hanging out with Crosby that Kiner ended up attending Hollywood parties and dating elite actresses, including Elizabeth Taylor, Ava Gardner, and Marilyn Monroe. In the 1950s and toward the end of his playing career, Kiner, who was born in California, returned to his native state with his new bride, tennis star Nancy Chaffe. He frequently told stories on air of attending glamorous parties, playing golf with Frank Sinatra and Bob Hope, and barbecuing with his neighbors, Lucille Ball and Desi Arnaz.

Kiner was forced to retire in 1956 due to chronic back pain. However, he immediately returned to baseball as general manager of the San Diego Padres, which at the time was the Triple A affiliate of the Cleveland Indians. As part of his job as general manager, Kiner had to broadcast the minor league team's games on radio. In 1961 his mentor from his rookie season with the Pirates, Hank Greenberg, was the general manager of the Chicago White Sox. Greenberg was impressed with Kiner's broadcasting skills and hired him to be part of their on-air broadcast team.

The next season in 1962, Kiner was hired away by the expansion Mets where he joined Bob Murphy and Lindsey Nelson to broadcast games on television. His contract included hosting *Kiner's Corner,* which he eventually changed to *Kiner's Korner* because he liked how the two Ks looked in back-to-back words. The show debuted on April 30, 1963, with "The Flag of Victory Polka" by Ira Ironstring playing over a simple graphic. Kiner sat politely, legs crossed, seated in one of two chairs. In his classic Hollywood style, Kiner opened the show with guests Buddy Hackett and Phil Foster, two popular comedians and actors during that era who had attended the game earlier that day.

Newsday sports media columnist Neil Best told Mark Rosenman and Howie Karpin, authors of the book *Down on the Korner,* that part of the show's success was because fans didn't get to interact with baseball players the way they can now. "At the time, it was invaluable because that was all we had," Best said. "Even if you watched the games back in that era, you weren't getting that many close-ups. [*Kiner's Korner*] was the only time you got to hear these players speak."

Episodes of Kiner's show typically ran 15 to 20 minutes. They were low-budget, casual, and in many cases, the guests were more in awe of Kiner than fans were in awe of the guest. Kiner, who had a 1940s-style dry sense of humor, would talk about the game, laugh, and recall moments from his career. His show was always entertaining but also educational because the viewer got to hear how baseball players talked about the game with a legendary hitter. "I loved going on *Kiner's Korner*," former Mets pitcher Dwight Gooden said in 2014. "I enjoyed talking baseball with Ralph, especially learning about players from his era. But what really made it special was every time you went on, you got $100. For a rookie like me in 1984, $100 was a big deal."

It was a sad day in baseball when Kiner passed away in February of 2014 at the age of 91. I'm a baseball fan in large part because of how Kiner and his play-by-play partner, Tim McCarver, explained Mets games on WOR-TV in the 1980s. The duo narrated the ups and downs of this franchise and led to my love affair with baseball. Sadly, many of the earliest episodes of *Kiner's Korner* were taped over. Tape was expensive in the 1960s and often re-used by production companies the next season.

Thankfully, in 2010 SNY.TV made classic episodes of the program available online, combining clips of classic interviews with updated discussions between him and host Ted Berg, who was 29 years old at the time of filming. "Sitting next to Ralph, hearing his voice in person was amazing enough on its own since I grew up listening to him. But his recall and his knowledge of the game were incredible," Berg told me about the experience. "He could remember pitch sequences from the 1950s. Also, even in his old age, he maintained some of the bravado of an all-time great hitter. He wasn't bragging or arrogant or anything. He just knew he'd been there. After I introduced him as 'Hall of Famer Ralph Kiner,' for about the seventh straight time that day, I asked if being introduced that way ever got old. He replied, 'How could that ever get old?'"

Kiner is a legend. He was there with us for Tom Seaver and "Ya Gotta Believe." He was there in 1986 and then through Mike Piazza and Matt Harvey. He saw and talked about it all. Despite dealing with Bell's palsy and slightly slurred speech, Kiner continued broadcasting. Toward the end of his career, which officially ended in 2013, he would occasionally join the broadcast booth during weekend games on SNY and WPIX.

Kiner's tenure with the Mets (1962–2013) made him the third longest tenured broadcaster in baseball history, trailing only Los Angeles Dodgers announcers Vin Scully (1950–2016) and Jaime Jarrin (1959–present). Kiner romanticized the game, telling stories that combined baseball and Hollywood in a way I never knew existed. He made me feel like, as a young fan, I was part of a legacy. He talked about hitting, technique, race, life on the road, personalities, aging, success and failure, and everything in between.

. . . .

Re-watch 1986 Mets— A Year to Remember Again and Again

Bucket Rank: 🗑️ 🗑️ 🗑️ 🗑️ 🗑️

Inspired by what NFL Films had been doing to document football games in the early 1980s, Major League Baseball Productions began producing year-ending documentaries in 1986, which were designed to chronicle a team's entire season. In November of

1986, they released the 60-minute documentary, *1986 Mets—A Year to Remember*. The VHS presented in story form—with narration, highlights, comedic bits, and player profiles set to popular music—the ups and downs of the franchise's entire world championship season.

It was—without question—the most-watched video tape in my house during the late 1980s. It would be an understatement to say I watched it multiple times per week. Thank you, Mom and Dad, for being among the first people on our block to buy a VCR.

The video's producer, David Israel, was a 24-year-old Mets fan, who would eventually find himself in the team's clubhouse, filming while they popped champagne and celebrated their success. "When you worked at MLB Productions, you got assigned to work on projects about different teams," he told *The New York Times* in 2016. "You did your job and you were happy to do your job, but you didn't necessarily love it. But the bosses tried—when they could—to put you on teams that you loved because it would bring out the passion. And to work on a Mets highlight film when they were winning was the greatest."

With the team's approval, the video's production group followed the Mets from spring training in St. Petersburg, Florida, through the final out of the World Series at Shea Stadium. The postgame clubhouse celebrations, in particular, are amazing because ordinarily during that era, all that we have of these moments for posterity is whatever was shown on the TV broadcast. However, in the case of the 1986 Mets, thanks to Israel and his colleagues, Mets fans get to see an up-and-close and personal, raw look at how their favorite team enjoyed the spoils of victory.

It's nice to see celebrations and highlights; that's important to a year-end video. However, what makes *A Year to Remember* most unique is how open the players were to working with the production team. This allowed the video to be more than just a reel of special on-field moments from an exciting season. Instead, in addition to the standard

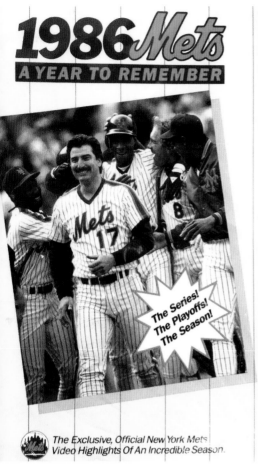

Every Mets fans needs to find a copy of 1986 Mets—A Year to Remember.
(Matthew Cerrone)

coverage, the film also includes a series of player-driven segments and profile videos set to popular music from that era.

The production team used Duran Duran's "Wild Boys" for a segment about the aggressive way Lenny Dykstra and Wally Backman played the game. Bob Seger's "Like a Rock" captured the veteran leadership and tough sensibility of Gary Carter and Keith Hernandez. Emerson Lake & Palmer's "Karn Evil No. 9" helped tell of the relaxed, confident way the Mets handled themselves on field. And Glenn Frey's "You Belong to the City" was used to show how New York embraced the ballclub's personalities on a level that transcended just baseball.

The most memorable vignette features reliever Roger McDowell and infielder Howard Johnson explaining how to make the perfect hot foot, a prank that ended with a teammate's shoe catching fire in the dugout or bullpen during a game. In the segment, which was filmed in the players' lounge at Shea Stadium during a rain delay, McDowell unrolls a wad of gum from his mouth onto the hot foot to use as an adhesive, while Johnson gazes at him, marveling at the relief pitcher's skill and attention to detail. "How does he do it?" Johnson asked quietly, so not to disturb the master. McDowell stopped with gum still unfolding from his mouth, looked up, and said, "Mirrors."

The video concludes with the Mets winning the World Series. However, it's the re-telling of Game 6, which was produced by Bob Klug, that becomes the 60-minute film's most compelling segment. For the most part, because of the team's dominant, regular-season success, the documentary is a fun, colorful, upbeat string of events with each one better than the next. The mood shifts, though, when the Red Sox take a 3–2 lead in the World Series.

Here, Klug adjusts to a dramatic, darker, more tenuous tone, capturing the mesmerizing tension that only baseball can create. It all leads up to the moment Mookie Wilson hits a ground ball through Bill Buckner's legs and the Mets win. As expected, the film picks up pace again.

However, the segment ends with Klug replaying the error with an echo added to the announcer's call, suggesting the moment will live on in baseball lore forever, which is exactly what happened.

I may not own a VCR anymore, but the documentary is so important to my childhood that I still have my original copy complete with its pinstripe cover and hard, enormous clamshell case. The film still holds up well 30 years later. It's particularly fun to watch with casual baseball fans, who may not know the intricacies of that specific team. And, of course, I get to relive some amazing moments from my days falling in love with baseball.

According to a survey I conducted on Twitter, 68 percent of my followers said they had seen *1986 Mets—A Year To Remember*. This is particularly impressive to me because more than 65 percent of Twitter's users are reportedly under 50 years old, meaning most of my poll's voters were likely kids, maybe younger, when the documentary was released. "I grew up in a family of Yankees fans, but my aunt married a die-hard Mets fan. It wasn't until the early '90s after the run of the late '80s Mets was over that my Uncle Frank started taking me to Mets games and telling me stories of the glory years that I had just missed," Mets fan Chris Olivieri, 33, from Staten Island, New York, told me. "One day while I was visiting my aunt and uncle, I found a handful of Mets VHS tapes, including *1986 Mets: A Year to Remember*. Watching it and seeing that team and their energy, the way that Shea literally shook, I was hooked. I wanted to see them do that in person some day. He let me keep the video, and I wore it out."

The thing I love best about the documentary, though, is that it is 100 percent about baseball and the team's success playing it. That's it. Today any time someone does a feature on the 1986 Mets, it is cluttered with salacious stories about partying, fights, and how their success ended too soon due to their off-field frailties. However, at the time the video was recorded—in real time, as the season was occurring—most of those sensational stories had yet to be reported. Therefore, the final product does a terrific job capturing exactly how I remember experiencing that year as it happened.

Checklist

CHECKLIST

Things to Know

- [ ] #LOLMets
- [ ] Laugh with the Comedians Who Are Mets Fans
- [ ] Get Duped by Sidd Finch
- [ ] Learn About Davey Johnson and the '86 Mets
- [ ] Understand Why Hodges Belongs in the Hall of Fame
- [ ] Learn About the Other Mr. Met

Things to Do

- [ ] Believe!
- [ ] Cheer with Cowbell Man
- [ ] Eat at Citi Field
- [ ] Attend Mets Fantasy Camp
- [ ] Fist Bump Mr. Met
- [ ] Grow a Mustache Like Keith Hernandez
- [ ] Experience the 7 Line
- [ ] Learn a Lesson from Bill Buckner
- [ ] Name Your Kid Shea
- [ ] Run the Mr. Met Dash
- [ ] Tour Citi Field
- [ ] Throw Out the First Pitch
- [ ] Go to a Playoff Game at Citi Field
- [ ] Catch a T-Shirt from the Party Patrol
- [ ] Go to Opening Day
- [ ] Be Terrific Like Tom Seaver
- [ ] Enjoy Some New York-Style Piazza

Places to Go

☐ Visit Cooperstown

☐ Go to a Brooklyn Cyclones Game

☐ Tour the Mets Hall of Fame and Museum

☐ Meet a Friend at the Apple

☐ See the Mets on the Road

☐ Go to Spring Training

☐ Visit the Bases from Shea

Things to Hear

☐ Get Metsmerized

☐ Learn Stengelese

☐ Listen to Bob Murphy

☐ Meet the Mets

☐ Chant "Let's Go Mets"

Things to Read

☐ Check Out *The Bad Guys Won*

☐ Learn About Alderson in *Baseball Maverick*

☐ Click on MetsBlog.com

☐ Learn the Game from Keith Hernandez's *Pure Baseball*

☐ Pick Up a Copy of *The Worst Team Money Could Buy*

☐ Relive *The Year the Mets Lost Last Place*

Things to See

☐ Log On to #MetsTwitter

☐ Watch *Kiner's Korner*

☐ Re-watch *1986 Mets—A Year to Remember* Again and Again

Acknowledgments

Thank you to this book's publisher, Triumph Books; my editor, Jeff Fedotin; and my literary agent, Stacey Glick. I have turned down countless book opportunities since starting MetsBlog.com in 2003. However, this one immediately felt right and would not have been completed had it not been for your expertise, guidance, and encouragement along the way.

Thank you to my friend and research assistant on this project, Meredith Perri. I first met Meredith when she interned for MetsBlog in 2012. She was smart, self-aware, and driven back then and she's smart, more aware, and more motivated today. The sky is the limit for Meredith, and it was an honor to get to work with her again.

Thank you, David Wright, for penning the foreword to this book. David and I first met in New Britain, Connecticut, when he was playing for Double A Binghamton. He doesn't remember this, nor should he. So I reintroduced myself in person a few years later in Port St. Lucie, Florida, where we coincidentally ended up having dinner together at a hibachi restaurant. His friends and my cousin talked NFL, fantasy sports, careers, and life as young men, and it helped create a trust that continues today.

Thank you to Fred Harner and Steve Raab at SNY, who I partnered with in 2007 to further develop MetsBlog. I know I'm not easy to work with. I know I'm neurotic and manic and never stop hustling. But it's born out of a love for the site, Mets fans, and a need to be fulfilled and moving forward. Fred and Steve do a great job putting up with me, and I look forward to generating more clicks together.

Thank you to my mom, Maryjane, who was not into baseball when I was born. She pushed me into Little League in hopes that I would make friends. I did. I was good at the game and I kept playing and learning, and she kept watching and learning with me. We became a Mets family. She and her friend, Alicia, would regularly leave work early and surprise me and Alicia's son, Joey, who was my best friend, with impromptu trips to Shea Stadium. We'd stay late, wait for autographs in the parking lot, and get home at ungodly hours, but we always had fun. She nurtured my love of baseball and helped make me a Mets fan.

Thank you to my dad, Michael, who passed away before this book was published. When I was a kid, he used to tape the final score of the previous night's game on my bedroom door so I knew the result the minute I got out of bed. He would use orange and blue markers, draw cartoons of the players, and make each clip unique. He and I rekindled our relationship in the late 1990s after he invited me to live with him in Massachusetts. He stopped watching baseball after divorcing my mom, but I got him back in through cheering Mike Piazza and Bobby Valentine. In time he became as big of a die-hard fan as I am. He helped me drop MetsBlog flyers on cars in the Shea Stadium parking lot, introduced me to helpful technology, and pushed me to keep innovating when I started to get stagnant. He nurtured my love of media and technology and helped make me a Mets blogger.

Thank you to my two daughters and my wife, Dorian, all of whom spend countless hours every day waiting for me to make one last post. My wife's patience and support are the secret ingredient to MetsBlog. Without it, nothing I do today in my professional life would be possible. If she had a nickel for every idea I've come up with in the last 20 years, she could retire tomorrow. Thankfully, because of her love and encouragement and her example of what it means to work hard for the right reasons, at least one of my ideas took flight.

Lastly, thank you, Mets fans and the readers of MetsBlog. You mean the world to me, and I'm very thankful for everyone who enjoys what I do. I don't see myself as a journalist. Instead, I know I'm in the business of customer service, keeping people aware and in the loop of what's going on with the Mets, offering context and insight from the perspective of a passionate fan. We're the same because we all want the Mets to win. Sure, we may disagree on the best ways for them to do this, but we all agree on the goal. When I started MetsBlog as a hobby, I never imagined writing it for the next 13 years and that it would become my full-time job. I love every minute of it and can't thank you enough for continuing to read and support my work.

Sources

Wire Services
Associated Press

Newspapers
The New York Times
Queens Gazette
The Wall Street Journal
New York Post
New York Daily News
Chicago Tribune

Magazines
People magazine
PC magazine
Sports Illustrated
Rolling Stone

TV/Radio/Film
ABC News
WPIX-TV
WBZ-TV
MLB Network
WFAN 660 AM
Seinfeld
I'm Keith Hernandez
The Howard Stern Radio Show
Let's Go Mets, Vestron Video
"Get Metsmerized," Passport Records
WOR 710 AM's *Mets On Deck*
The Daily Show with Jon Stewart
1986 Mets—A Year To Remember, Rainbow Home Video

Websites

Mets.com

Metsblog.com

Timesunion.com

Tcpalm.com

ABCnews.com

USATODAY.com

ESPN.com

SNY.TV.com

Forbes.com

AOL.com

Bleacherreport.com

Traditionfield.com

SI.com

Dailybeast.com

Victoryjournal.com

Baseball-reference.com

FOXSports.com

Talkingchop.com

Isys6621.com

Books

Silverman, Matthew. *Best Mets: Fifty Years of Highs and Lows from New York's Most Agonizingly Amazin' Team.* Taylor Trade Publishing (2014)

Shaughnessy, Dan. *At Fenway: Dispatches from Red Sox Nation.* Crown (2010)

Darling, Ron. *Game 7, 1986: Failure and Triumph in the Biggest Game of My Life.* St. Martin's Press (2016)

Pearlman, Jeff. *The Bad Guys Won: A Season of Brawling, Boozing, Bimbo Chasing, and Championship Baseball with Straw, Doc, Mookie, Nails, the Kid, and the Rest of the...on a New York Uniform—and Maybe the Best.* Harper-Collins (2009)

Kettman, Steve. *Baseball Maverick: How Sandy Alderson Revolutionized Baseball and Revived the Mets.* Atlantic Monthly Press (2015)

Hernandez, Keith. *Pure Baseball.* Harper Perennial (1995)

Klapisch, Bob; Harper, John. *The Worst Team Money Could Buy.* Bison Books (1993)

Paul Zimmerman, Paul; Schaap, Dick. *The Year the Mets Lost Last Place.* Signet (1969)

Rosenman, Mark; Karpin, Howie. *Down on the Korner: Ralph Kiner and Kiner's Korner.* Carrel Books (2016)

Reports

Robert Wood Johnson Foundation and the Harvard T.H. Chan School of Public Health's report on Sports and Health in America (2014)

American Mustache Institute's Top Sports Mustache of All Time (2007)

U.S. Census (2010)

Social Security Administration name search (1969)